Sunderland
—a short—
History

Tom Corfe

Albion
Press

Albion Press
40 Park Parade Roker Sunderland Tyne & Wear
ISBN 0 9525122 3 8

First published 1973 by Frank Graham
This edition published 2003

For more information on other Albion Press titles
access http://members.tripod.co.uk/albionpress

© Tom Corfe, 1973, 2003

The right of Tom Corfe to be identified as
author of this work has been asserted by him in
accordance with the Copyright, Designs and Patents Act 1988

Cover photograph by Shaun Dodds

Typeset and designed by UpStyle Book Design
www.upstyle.co.uk
Printed and bound in Great Britain
by Biddles Limited of King's Lynn

Contents

Foreword to Second Edition 4
Foreword 5
At the Mouth of the Wear 7
The Monks 13
The Villagers 18
The Growing Port 22
One Town 33
'A Very Large Ship-Building, Coaly Town' 50
The Twentieth Century 69
Table of Recent Dates 89
Note on Sources 90
Index 93
Picture Credits 96

Foreword to Second Edition

In recent years the number of books on Sunderland has increased greatly and a wide variety of publications is available to anyone interested in the city's past. But when Tom Corfe's book first appeared in 1973 this was not the case. At that time the most significant recent contribution was a book entitled *Some Chapters on the History of Sunderland* (published in 1969) which was edited, financed and partly written by Helen G. Bowling, a former teacher at Sunderland Church High School.

One of the contributors to Helen's book was Tom Corfe. An avid historian, Tom had settled in Sunderland in 1962 to take up a post at Sunderland Teacher Training College, and soon began developing a keen interest in local history when taking students on guided walks around the town.

Although welcome, *Some Chapters* was not a continuous history of Sunderland, and thus not long after its publication Tom Corfe eagerly took on the challenge of writing such a book for the Newcastle-based publisher Frank Graham who, in due course, produced an attractive volume. Corfe's book, *Sunderland: a Short History*, was enthusiastically received and the print run of at least 1,000 copies sold out within two years. Given that no general history of the town had appeared for several decades, Corfe's work might well have proved successful even if the text were nondescript. But this is not the case. All in all, it is a good book, an appealing blend of learning and lucidity by an able and conscientious scholar.

I wish to thank Frank Graham for very kindly granting permission for the book to be republished. For this edition, with Tom Corfe's approval, I have appended a table of recent dates to the text and have updated the bibliography.

It only remains to thank Tom Corfe for writing the book in the first place. I read it for the first time when I was about 12, and have retained affection and respect for it ever since. It is a valuable contribution to the literature on Sunderland and will no doubt be read for many years to come.

Glen Lyndon Dodds
Sunderland, 29 October 2003

Foreword

IT is more than fifty years since there was last a continuous history of Sunderland. That is the main justification for attempting this summary, on the eve of Sunderland's disappearance as an independent borough. It is an attempt to put together what has been written on the town in a variety of books, pamphlets and periodicals, and link it to what is still visible on the ground. It cannot lay claim to any great originality, and its debt to those previous writers listed in the bibliography will be plain to any who have read them. I am only too well aware of the traps awaiting an outsider, a Sunderland resident for no more than ten years, who tries to write on the town; and I regret that no native better equipped than I am to write this book has seen fit to do so.

The story necessarily has many gaps, and leaves many questions unanswered. It is to be hoped that the many aspects of Sunderland's past that would repay examination and re-examination will receive the attention they deserve in the near future.

Apart from the writers whose work I have pillaged, I must thank all who have saved me from at least some of my errors and have helped in many other ways. They include Mrs Helen G. Bowling, Miss M. A. S. Hickmore, Mr L. P. Crangle and Mr H. L. Robson; Mr J. W. Haldane, Mr J. H. Wilson and their colleagues at Sunderland Museum; the staff of the Central Library and of the Durham Record Office; the officials of the Planning, Architect's, and Public Relations departments of the Corporation and of the Port of Sunderland Authority; the editor and photographic librarian of the *Sunderland Echo*; my colleagues at Sunderland College of Education and many students, whose researches I have been able to utilize; and my wife who has helped throughout, and has been responsible for all the maps and drawings.

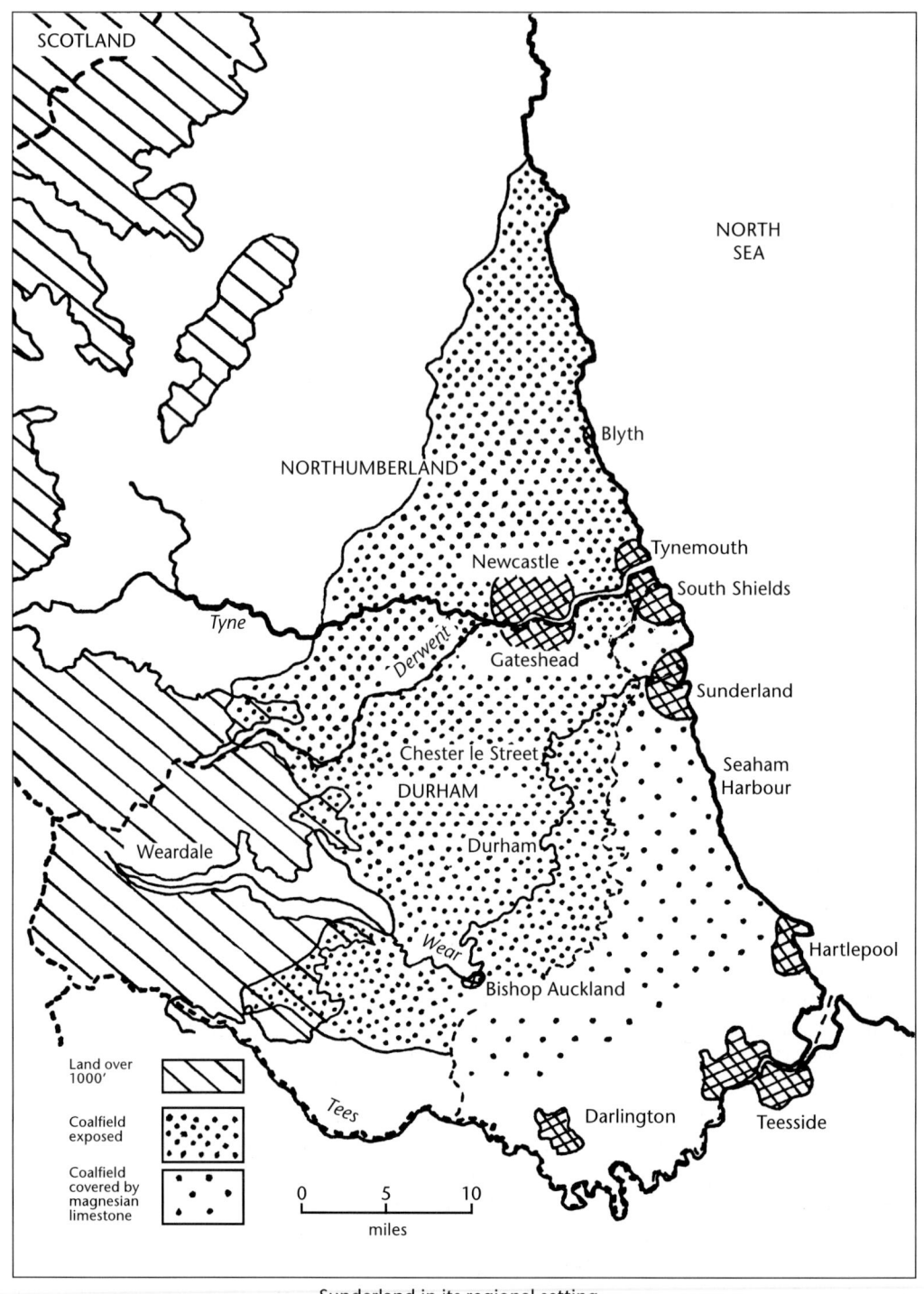

Sunderland in its regional setting

Chapter One

At the Mouth of the Wear

THE River Wear rises at the western tip of the triangle that is County Durham. From the windswept Pennine moorlands and soggy peat hags it flows eastwards through the grey and green of Weardale, with its quarries, stone villages, long-abandoned lead workings. The valley slopes become gentler and the river grows, until it emerges fully-fledged through the foothills beyond Wolsingham. At this point it seems to forget its original intention of bisecting the county by heading direct for the North Sea; it starts to wander southwards instead as though in search of the Tees. But at Bishop Auckland it changes again, swinging to the north and winding by way of a gravelly flood plain and deep-cut meanders across the central lowlands of Durham. Now the Tyne seems to be its objective.

At times in its remote prehistory, long before the memory of man, the Wear indeed found its outlet through one or other of these rival rivers, the rivers that now mark Durham's southern and northern boundaries. In the later millennia of the great Ice Ages, when the main sheet had melted but congested ice-masses still blocked many valleys, the Wear formed a broad, shallow lake in what is now the plain of central Durham. To the east it was held in by the shelf of magnesian limestone that can be seen today so clearly where the Durham road rises from Houghton-le-Spring. But the Wear lake found its outlet eventually not to north or south but over that very limestone, breaking out eastwards from where Chester-le-Street now stands. Abandoning its older channels, now packed with ice and silt, the river wore a gorge into the rock and so at last burst out into the North Sea.

At its outlet, the limestone plateau is about a hundred feet above the sea. It rises higher in a few exposed, rocky knolls; Building Hill, Tunstall Hill, Hasting Hill, Humbledon Hill, Carley Hill are among the most notable. At its seaward edge the plateau grades down to a thirty-foot cliff of boulder clay. A dozen streamlets once fell from the plateau into the river or the sea, carving tiny, steep-walled valleys; but many have now disappeared into culverts.

'Wearmouth', Sunderland has been called for most of its history, and 'Wear mouth' best describes the origin and nature of the town. Between Shields and Hartlepool the Durham coast is not a hospitable one; an almost featureless stretch of limestone and crumbling clay, it stands exposed to easterly gales. There are no natural havens, and only a few shallow coves like that of Dalden, where nineteenth century enterprise and engineering carved out Seaham Harbour. The mouth of the Wear for long provided the only substantial anchorage, and that was never an easy one. Where the river's flow and the North Sea tides met, sand and mud were deposited to form a shifting blockage to the channel and a bar that made entry hazardous. The winds that whipped the North Sea into a white fury all too often blew from the north-east and reached unhindered into the lower stretches of the river to wreak havoc on anchored vessels. Sandbanks, tides, cliffs all hampered the landing and lading of cargoes.

The communities about the Wear mouth that merged at last to become Sunderland first came to life during the 'Dark Ages' of Anglo-Saxon England. But thousands of years before the continuous history of their development began, men were living around the river mouth; and we can find their traces today on the ground or in the cases of the museum.

They are not very substantial traces. Apart from the fact that eastern Durham has, in the last two centuries of intensive industrial development, largely obliterated the remnants of its prehistoric past, the region never seems to have been very thickly populated. Of the earliest men, the Palaeolithic hunters, there is virtually no trace, for the North-East remained bleakly ice-bound through much of their era. In Mesolithic times, perhaps 9,000 years ago, groups of skilled hunting, fishing people built semi-permanent camps on the shoreline, making themselves finely worked implements of flint and bone. A scatter of tiny microliths and a single axe from Monkwearmouth attest their presence. Their Neolithic successors, perhaps about 3000 B.C., were the folk who first hacked and burnt clearings in the forest, scratched at the soil, tended cattle and sheep. Of that revolutionary change in human history there is little trace in this corner of County Durham; only a burial at Copt Hill near Houghton-le-Spring, and a few scattered polished axeheads. The first people who knew anything of metal, those we call the Beaker Folk, seem to have invaded from across the North Sea and found their way up the rivers; but the Wear in its stony gorge did not encourage their penetration as the Tyne did. Nevertheless one of their descendants was buried on Hasting Hill, in a grave cut into the limestone, lined and covered with slabs of sandstone. Four thousand years later, in 1911, archaeologists opened the mound that covered him and found the skeleton crouched on its side. With it was the man's flint knife and the remnants of the meal meant to sustain him in the after-life: the bones of some fish and an earthenware beaker to hold his beer.

The Bronze Age people who came after him re-used the burial mound on Hasting Hill time and again. Over the centuries other bodies were placed in it; sometimes they too were in stone-lined graves, accompanied by food vessels or other offerings; sometimes, when religious beliefs and practices had changed, their bodies were cremated. Not far away is Humbledon Hill, a similar limestone knoll. Here, when the reservoir was built in 1873, three large urns of the Middle Bronze Age (perhaps 1000 B.C.) were uncovered. Each was stuffed with fragments of cremated bone.

We have a good deal of evidence about the Bronze Age people's way of death, though little, unfortunately, on their life. We have one relic, however, of their speech. These settlers by the river gave it a name: 'water', they called it, quite simply; 'visur' it was, or something very similar, in their pre-Celtic language. 'Visur' it has remained, though the millennia have transformed the word into the modern 'Wear'. On the far side of the North Sea relatives of those ancient people, speaking the same unknown language, named another river similarly; today it is the German Weser.

In the following centuries the record for this region is an almost complete blank. In A.D. 71 the Romans swept north, overrunning the great tribal confederacy of the Brigantes, whose headquarters were in modern Yorkshire. These hardy people

At the Mouth of the Wear

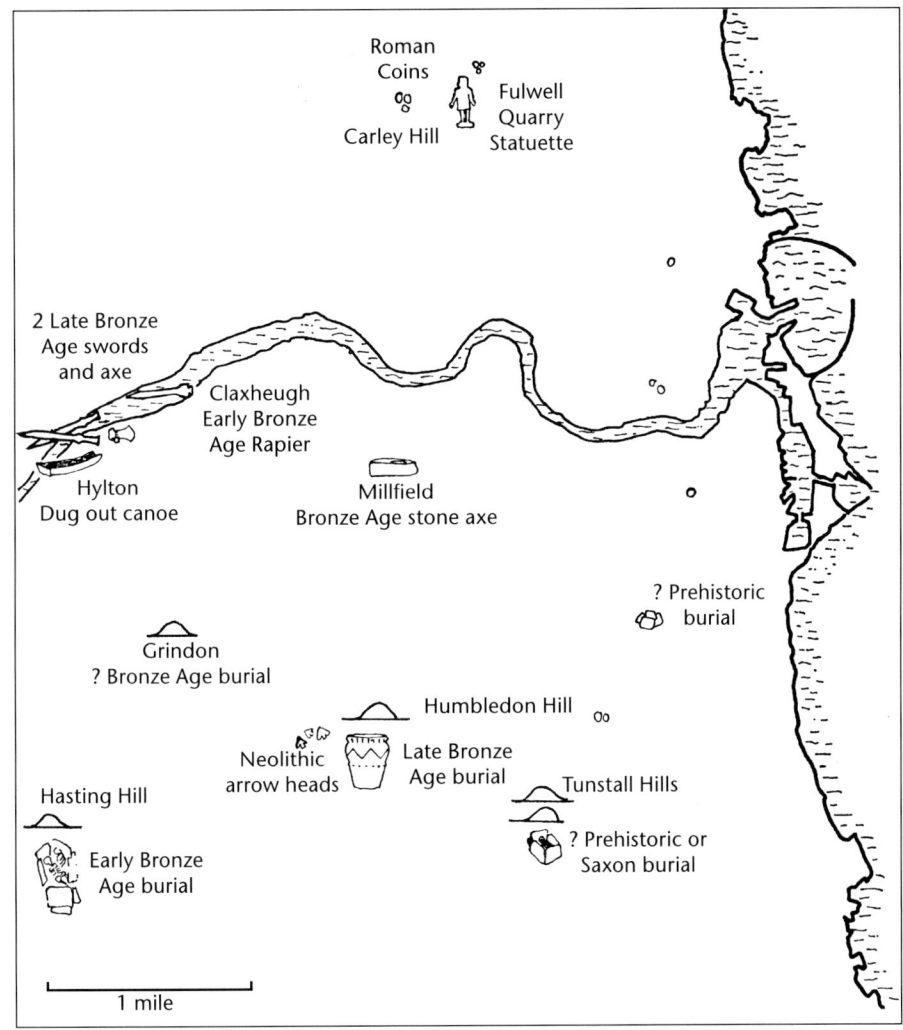

Major Prehistoric and Roman discoveries in the Sunderland area

were keepers of cattle and sheep, living in scattered family communities. Eastern Durham seems to have been dotted with their farms, palisaded and ditched enclosures big enough to shelter the cattle by night. Almost every trace of these farmsteads has disappeared; only a few can be detected from the air as shadowy marks in the ripening crops.

The Romans brought no fundamental change to this pastoral way of life. Their occupation in the North-East was essentially a military presence, and there seems to have been no attempt at economic reorganization or exploitation. Roman legionaries and auxiliaries marched northwards to the great frontier system of Hadrian's Wall, to their vast base at Corstopitum (Corbridge) and to Caledonia beyond; but their route was along Dere Street, far away in the Pennine foothills, or perhaps by way of the later road to the Tyne crossing at Pons Aelius (Newcastle).

At first, it seems, the coastal region interested the Romans little. They had one major fort at Arbeia (South Shields) which was both a terminus to the Hadrianic frontier system and a supply base for maritime expeditions against the Pictish peoples to the north. Later, the threats of raiders from across the North Sea led to the building of fortified signal stations along the coast. Several of these are known from Yorkshire, the most northerly at Huntcliff, near Saltburn. Each consisted of a massive square tower, perhaps 80 or so feet high and 45 feet across, set in the middle of a square stone wall which had corner bastions to carry stone-throwing artillery; a ditch surrounded the whole.

It seems possible that some similar building was set up at or near Sunderland, placed on high ground with a good view along the coast. Certainly there is ample evidence of Roman presence in the neighbourhood. From time to time Roman coins have been found.

A Roman signal station. This is based on the remains of the station that stands on the cliff at Scarborough

A bronze statue of Jupiter emerged from a quarry at Carley Hill and what may be a Roman altar from the excavations at Monkwearmouth Church. But of buildings there is no definite trace. At various times it has been suggested that there was a Roman military building overlooking the river near the present Vaux's Brewery, a pottery on the Town Moor, a bridge at Hylton, and a road approaching from the south along the line of the present Stockton Road. In each case there is some archaeological evidence, but in no case is it conclusive; it badly needs re-examination and re-assessment by an expert.

If there was a signal station at Wearmouth there may well have been also a civil settlement, a small community of fishermen and farmers that supplied the garrison and perhaps continued long after the last repesentative of Rome was gone. We can do no more than guess at what happened around the mouth of the Wear in the two and a half centuries that followed the end of Roman Britain, though we know more of the coastlands to south and north. We know that Germanic peoples from across the North Sea were settling in strength in Yorkshire during the fifth century. We know that others, Angles from the Danish fenlands, were established along the Northumbrian coastline about Bamburgh by about 547, founding their own kingdom of Bernicia.

Some time late in the sixth century Anglian settlers probably arrived at the mouth of the Wear; but whether they came as allies of a local British prince or as aggressive raiders destroying villages and driving out the inhabitants we do not know. Probably they sought protection from, and owed allegiance to, the King of Bernicia. Perhaps it was some of these early settlers whose cremated remains were found early last century buried on the flank of Tunstall Hill. Perhaps it was one of them, Here, who settled with his family and followers at the 'Herings' farmstead'; but though 'Herrington' looks as though it implies an early settlement of this kind it may be misleading. The interpretation of local place-names depends very largely on guesswork since early written forms of the names rarely occur in Durham. Certainly many of the physical features in and near Wearmouth were given the names they still bear at some time during the Anglo-Saxon centuries. Humbledon Hill (the bare-topped hill?), Ryhope (the rough valley?), Whitburn (Hwita's barn or burialplace?), Hendon (the valley of the hinds?); in all these Anglo-Saxon descriptions have become fossilized as place-names. They offer tiny clues to the interests and activities of these early English farmers, building their homes of wood and wattle and thatch, clearing the woodland, ploughing and sowing on both sides of what they called the 'Were mutha'.

During the last decade of the sixth century much of north-eastern England was brought firmly under the control of the Bernician King Aethelfrith. His warriors overran many of the regions formerly held by the Britons and destroyed their armies in battle. Finally he gained control of the Yorkshire kingdom of Deira. When Aethelfrith died in 616 he had created a massive new kingdom, Northumbria; and it was under the kings of Northumbria that the communities of Wearmouth first emerged into history.

Sunderland–A Short History

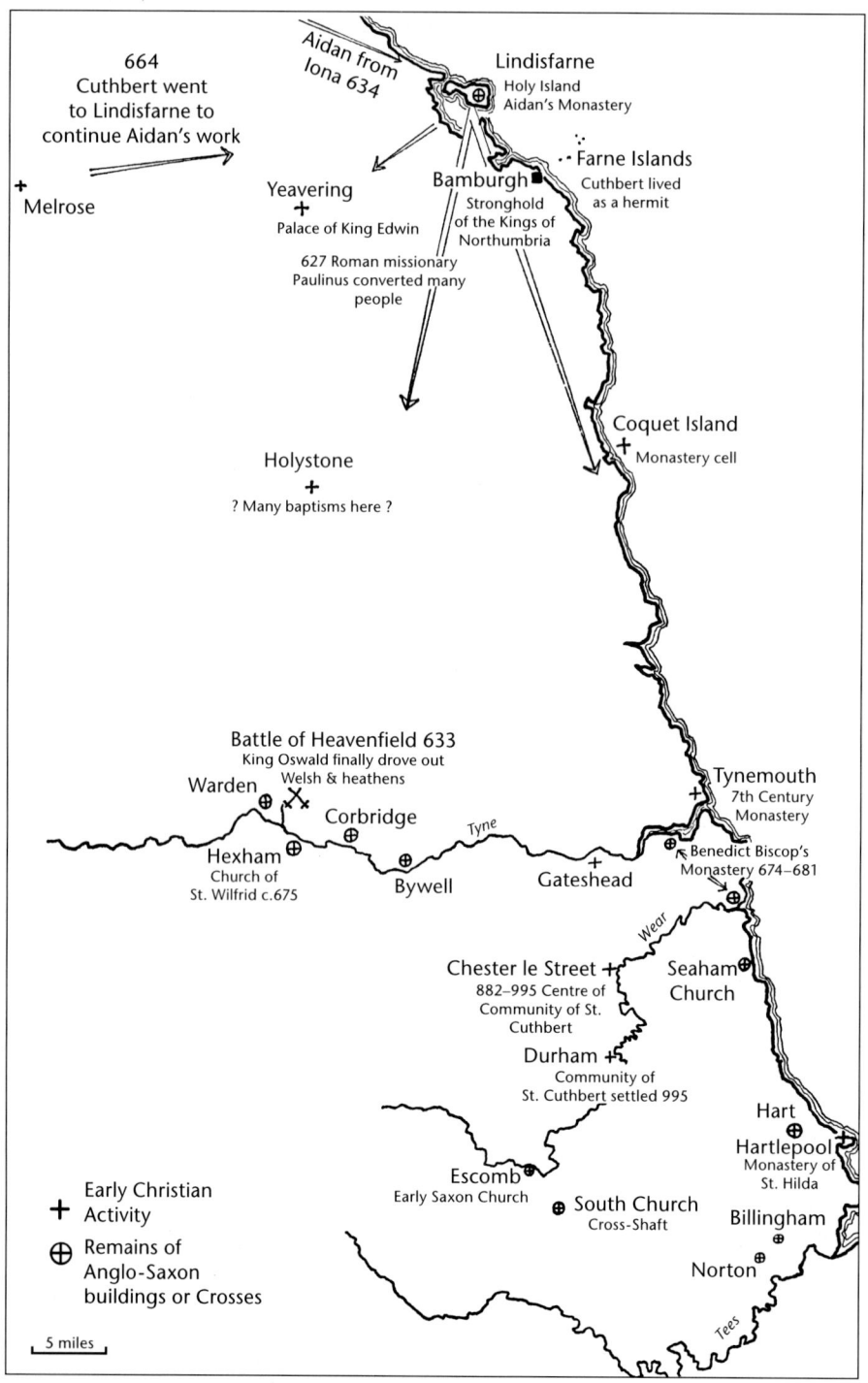

Early Christianity in Northumbria

Chapter Two

The Monks

UNTIL the last quarter of the seventh century everything that happened at Wearmouth is a matter of guesswork. Then, in the year 674 one of the communities that subsequently became Sunderland suddenly emerged into the full light of history. The first and perhaps the greatest of English historians, Bede, lived and worked throughout his life in or near Wearmouth. He has left us a vivid and detailed record of the settlement in his own lifetime.

'The pious servant of Christ, Biscop, called Benedict, with the assistance of the Divine grace, built a monastery in honour of the most holy of the apostles, St Peter, near the mouth of the river Were, on the north side,' says Bede. Benedict Biscop, a nobleman of the court of Northumbria, was wealthy and important, a friend of King Oswy himself. He was still a young man when a surge of enthusiasm for the newly-returned Christian faith swept through the Northumbrians. The saintly Aidan had come from the great Scottish monastery of Iona to establish himself and his followers on Lindisfarne, Holy Island. From there he conducted a vigorous missionary campaign to spread once more among the heathen Angles the doctrines of Christianity, doctrines long preserved among the Irish and carried by them to Iona. Inspired by the simplicity and earnestness of such men, young Benedict gave up what was, for the seventh century, a life of ease and pleasure to devote himself wholeheartedly and rigorously to the service of God and the Church.

But Benedict could never be a mere follower where others pointed the way. He possessed the independent outlook and enquiring mind of a high-born nobleman, together with the wealth and status to indulge it. He found little satisfaction in learning his faith at second hand from the simple monks of Holy Island. He set out to explore for himself every aspect of the Church of Christ; and he looked directly to Rome as the fountainhead of western Christianity rather than to the learned but isolated and outmoded scholar-monks of Ireland. He spent two years of study and prayer in the strict discipline of a Mediterranean monastery, and he travelled widely in Italy. He went on to Rome itself and there conferred with the Pope and with other leaders of the Church.

In the course of his several visits to Rome Benedict, bred among unsophisticated barbarians, saw for himself the splendours and mysteries of a great and ancient city. The magnificent buildings, elaborate ritual and sonorous music wherewith God was worshipped, so very different from the puritan simplicity of Holy Island, captured his imagination. It became Benedict's ambition to re-create something of this atmosphere in his far-off homeland.

Benedict returned to England at the Pope's behest in 668 to act as interpreter and guide to the newly appointed Archbishop of Canterbury, the Greek monk Theodore of Tarsus. For two years he headed a monastery at Canterbury, but in 674 he came back to Northumbria and persuaded the new king, Ecgfrith, to grant him the land he needed to support a foundation of his own. He was given seventy hides, perhaps fifteen square miles, on the north bank of the Wear. It may be that a settlement dating from Roman days still survived there; and it may have been near this spot that Aidan had, some twenty-five years before, established a small convent of nuns under the future St Hilda.

Benedict set himself an immense task. He sought to plant among a people who had barely emerged from barbarism the skills and traditions of a thousand-year-old civilization. He meant to erect, among folk who knew nothing of building in stone, a church modelled on those of Rome itself. He hoped to introduce those whose knowledge of music and writing was rudimentary to the most sophisticated forms of worship and learning. The simple huts of wood and wattle that the Northumbrians built for themselves, the huts that had sufficed for Aidan and his followers on Holy Island, did not satisfy Benedict's concept of a suitably purposeful setting for Christian worship. This remote backwater of Christendom was to reflect the splendours of Rome itself.

He needed all his determination, his wealth, and his wide range of contacts throughout Europe. From Gaul he brought skilled masons to supervise the construction of his church; and they did their work so well that some of it, the porch and part of the western wall, has survived countless destructive assaults and stood through thirteen centuries. Finely carved stone and vivid paintings of the Gospel story decorated the church, making its message clear to the humble folk who came to wonder and to learn. In time a majestic stone figure (though whether of St Peter or of Christ we do not know) was set in the gable above the porch. Continental glaziers came to teach local workmen their craft so that the monastery might be provided with windows and fine glass vessels. Other sacred vessels and rich vestments Benedict collected from the churches and monasteries of Europe on numerous journeys. In the same way he laid the foundations of a fine library, bringing many rare and costly books so that the monks of Wearmouth should never lack Christian learning.

As to the worship of God, that must be conducted according to the best possible practice. It was, after all, first and foremost for that purpose he proposed to educate some hundreds of his fellow-countrymen out of their uncouth ignorance. So Benedict persuaded the Pope to lend him no less a personage than John, the Arch-Chanter of St Peter's in Rome, who was then on a special mission from the Pope to the English bishops. No one in the whole of Christendom could have been better qualified to train the Wearmouth monks in the skilled business of singing the praises of God correctly.

It must have been a dazzling, awe-inspiring experience for the simple fisher-folk and farmers of Wearmouth to find a strange and beautiful building of stone rising in their midst, to observe the discipline and devotion of their fellows who had entered the monastic life, to hear daily the mysterious, splendid chanting and the unfamiliar words of the Latin ritual.

The whirlwind enthusiasm of Benedict was not limited to Wearmouth. By 681 he had received another grant of land from the king, forty hides a few miles away among the marsh-dwelling folk called the Gyrwe, where perhaps the Romans had once had another fort. There he set up, under his friend Ceolfrith, the second part of what now became a double monastery. The house of St Peter at Wearmouth was complemented by that of St Paul at Jarrow; and at Jarrow Ceolfrith's dedication stone, set up in 685, can still be read.

There was one other grant to come. From a sixth and final visit to Rome Benedict returned in 686 bringing among other treasures two finely worked silk cloaks as a present for King Aldfrith, Ecgfrith's successor. In return the king gave him three further hides of land, perhaps 400 acres, on the south bank of the Wear. It may be that this was the 'separate land' beyond the river, the 'Sunderland' that gave its name in time to the whole town; though it may be that the name is of much later origin.

Shortly before Benedict died in 689 he appointed his companion and friend Ceolfrith (pronounced Cholfrith) to be his successor. Ceolfrith had much in common with the founder. He too was a Northumbrian noble. He too directed the twin communities with wisdom and ability, and his rule lasted for twenty-eight years. We know a good deal about Ceolfrith for we have not only Bede's account but that of another, anonymous, admirer who also lived and worked under his guidance. Both wrote with the utmost respect for a revered master, so perhaps the portrait that emerges is an uncritical one; but there is no doubt that Ceolfrith proved a very worthy successor to Benedict Biscop.

Nobody can be sure how St Peter's looked in the days of Ceolfrith and Bede, but it may have been something like this

The monastery grew in size. There were 600 monks there by the time of Ceolfrith's death in 716, and Wearmouth must have seemed a great city of learning and craftsmanship in comparison with the tiny wooden hamlets about it. It was perhaps in Ceolfrith's time that the gabled roof and the great statue were added above the porch, and the monastic buildings beside the church were extended in stone, their cement floors built after the Roman fashion with powdered brick. Its reputation as the greatest centre of religion and learning in the Anglo-Saxon world was firmly established. Above all, the learned Bede, born somewhere near Wearmouth a year or so before the monastery's foundation, came to be respected as the supreme scholar of his age. His studies of, and commentaries on, the Scriptures were known throughout Christendom. He was widely read in authors both classical and Christian. He was spoken of as a brilliant teacher. And it was he who, weaving together the knowledge gleaned in a lifetime of reading and of contact with many of the great of his day, ordering it and interpreting it with skill and judgment, compiled the *Ecclesiastical History of the English People* that stands today as the foundation stone of English historical scholarship.

While Bede studied and wrote, Ceolfrith continued Benedict's work of building up the superb library needed to support such scholarship. Apart from the books that he, like his predecessor, brought from the continent, Ceolfrith had his monks copy out many rare volumes to stock its shelves. Above all he needed, as central items for the collection, complete copies of the Bible. He had indeed brought one back with him after a visit to Italy, but it was an outmoded translation, and one copy was in any case hardly sufficient for the hundreds of scholar-monks. He set the skilled copyists of the monastery scriptorium to produce three complete copies of the improved Latin translation that had been prepared by St Jerome. It was a formidable task that entailed years of careful work, but when at last the three Bibles were finished they became the monastery's proudest possessions, constantly in use at the two houses. When, at seventy-five, Ceolfrith decided to set out on a last pilgrimage to Rome he took with him one of the great Bibles as a present for the Pope. But it was a journey that Ceolfrith never completed; he died on the way.

Ninety years ago it was discovered that the Bible Ceolfrith had taken with him on that last journey still existed, treasured in a library at Florence. The Bible painstakingly prepared nearly 1,300 years ago at Wearmouth is today one of the most famous books in the world, known from the Italian monastery of Monte Amiato where it had long remained unrecognized, as the *Codex Amiatinus*. It is a huge volume; there are over 2,000 pages of vellum, each 14 inches by 20½ inches (36 by 52 cm.); it is ten inches thick; and it weighs more than five stone. To make it and its two fellows a vast herd of more than 1,500 calves were slaughtered so that their skins, stretched and pounded and scraped and smoothed, might provide a perfect surface for writing. Copied out clearly and beautifully in the hands of nine skilled scribes, decorated with a set of brilliantly coloured paintings, the *Codex* as it exists today reveals an extraordinary flowering of literary, artistic, and calligraphic craftsmanship in Anglo-Saxon England.

The monastery of St Peter and St Paul continued to prosper through much of the eighth century, but with its close came the savage attacks of the Vikings. The long, unsheltered coast, so often exposed to fierce north-easterly gales, now suffered from the far more lethal threat of the sea-rovers. Wearmouth, like Jarrow and Lindisfarne, naturally attracted attention. The wood and wattle huts of the villagers were burnt, and many must have died violently. The stout stonework of Benedict and Ceolfrith survived, though in a roofless and ruinous state. The monastery, the pride of Northumbria's golden age, finally came to an end in 870; but the church still continued in use, and many victims of those miserable years were buried around it. The building was restored and re-roofed about 900, when the fury had passed; and perhaps it was at this time that a slender tower was raised on the ruins of the old porch.

A few decades later destruction came yet again to Wearmouth. This time a different enemy swept into the vulnerable North-East, an enemy whose depredations were to affect profoundly the region's development over the next five centuries. In 1070, in the chaos and internecine conflict that followed the Norman invasion, the Scottish armies of King Malcolm ravaged through Northumbria, and once again the church of St Peter was almost totally destroyed.

When the Scots had gone the North settled down under the firm grip of King William's lieutenants. Chief among them was the Bishop of Durham, who now began to appear in the position he held throughout the Middle Ages as all-powerful viceroy in the troubled, remote borderlands. Life came back to the church by the river mouth. A surge of monastic revival, reinforced by the new continental influences brought by the Normans, reached the North-East. Momentarily it seemed as though St Peter's might once again become a centre of enlightenment and civilization. Monks arrived to clear away the brambles and thornbushes that overran the crumbled walls, to create a new community. But now Wearmouth was overshadowed by the great bulk of Durham, secure on its rocky, fortified peninsula from the assaults to which the older church had been so long exposed.

It was at Durham that the monks of St Cuthbert, driven by Vikings from their Holy Island home, had finally settled. It was here that the Norman Bishops Palatine, the Prince-Bishops wielding royal authority and enjoying rich incomes, built their castle and their massive new cathedral, establishing a monastery of Benedictines. For the Benedictine monks of Durham St Peter's now became an outlying cell, occupied by a few monks (sometimes only two) under a 'master'. There they played, for more than four centuries, a small but active part in the life and commerce of the people about the river mouth. So the lands that had once been granted to Benedict Biscop passed into the possession of the new Norman monastery at the cathedral of Durham, and the northern bank of the river came in time to be known as the Monks' lands, Monkwearmouth.

Chapter Three

The Villagers

IN contrast to the very full picture we can draw of the early days at Monkwearmouth, we know little about the settlements south of the river, the lands that belonged not to the monastery but to the Bishop himself. His right derived from the somewhat unlikely story that as long ago as 930 King Athelstan had granted extensive territories and many villages to the community of St Cuthbert. Among these, Wearmouth was specifically named, and the Bishop asserted his claim as heir to all the lands of St Cuthbert. It was a claim that no one in the twelfth century would be likely to oppose. It may well be that a village had indeed existed at the time of Athelstan, or even before it; but there is no reliable evidence for it before the end of the twelfth century.

The village that came to be known as Bishopwearmouth occupied a low hill-top about one hundred feet above the level of the river, a mile up from the sandbanks at its mouth and the monastery on the far shore. Eastwards the land sloped gently to the coast. To the north limestone cliffs overlooked the river. Southwards the hill extended into a ridge running up to the stony outcrop of Building (or Bildon, or Boyldon) Hill, while on the west was a streamlet that came to be called the Howle-Eile Burn, passing through a steepsided little valley and later crossed by the hind's bridge carrying the road out westwards.

It was on the bank some twenty feet above this burn that the building of St Michael's Church was begun early in the thirteenth century, probably to replace an older wooden building. North of the church was the glebe land of the rector, where in later years a substantial stone rectory was built. South of it was the village green, about which the peasants' cottages stood, perhaps laid out in the orderly fashion imposed upon most of the Bishop's villages.

About 1183 Bishop Hugh de Puiset caused a detailed inventory of his lands and tenants to be compiled. It has become known as Boldon Book, for that village is described first and in full detail. Boldon Book provides us with a portrait of Bishopwearmouth at this early stage in its history, but it is unfortunately a sketchy and confusing one. An important element of the population, those who were free and therefore owed no services to the Bishop, were completely omitted. For the purposes of the Bishop's rentals Bishopwearmouth was linked with the outlying hamlet of Tunstall (whose name means simply 'the farmstead'), two miles to the south. Between them there were twenty-two villeins, the same number as dwelt in Boldon itself and fewer than those in, for example, Easington (with thirty-one). Each villein held two oxgangs (perhaps thirty acres) of land, for which he paid rents and dues in kind (oats, chickens, eggs, loads of wood) and in money as well as labouring for three days a week on the Bishop's own lands. There were six cottagers with smaller holdings, and in addition a carpenter, a smith, and a pinder charged with responsibility for strayed animals.

But in addition to this farming community there was another settlement on the south bank of the river, a fishing village facing the monastery on that stretch of land known as Sunderland. Sometimes this settlement was referred to as 'the port of Wearmouth', and it was generally regarded as an outlying hamlet attached to the Bishop's village, part of the parish of St Michael but separated from the main vill. This may indeed represent another possible origin of the name, which seems to have come into use at about the time of Boldon Book; and the Book has a brief reference to 'Sunderland', though it may refer to the hamlet of Sunderland Bridge, near Croxdale.

Hugh de Puiset, an ambitious and strong-willed Bishop, was anxious to promote the wealth and strength of his Palatinate lands. He sought, like so many of the magnates of his age, to create new boroughs. Those who dwelt in boroughs enjoyed freedom and privileges not granted to the humble peasant. Skilled craftsmen and busy merchants, attracted to an environment so congenial for their talents and enterprise, might be expected to yield their sponsor a handsome return in tolls and dues. Moreover the Palatinate lacked a satisfactory outlet for its commerce; to the north the royal borough of Newcastle was already beginning to demonstrate how a port might grow in these neglected northern parts, basing its success on exports of wool and, later, coal.

So about the time when Boldon Book was being compiled Bishop Hugh chartered a borough of his own: Wearmouth. It is not clear whether the charter was directed simply to the community at the river mouth or whether it embraced the mother settlement about the parish church. The charter took care to deal with the interests and responsibilities of a farming community as well as those concerned with trade. As it was to rival the growing port on the Tyne, Wearmouth's new burgesses were granted the same rights and privileges that those of Newcastle already enjoyed. They might hold their own civil courts to settle matters of debt; they might, under certain restrictions, trade with any vessel calling at the port; they had hereditary right to hold or sell their lands; they were freed from liability to pay certain traditional fines and dues to the Bishop; they might own private handmills and ovens, cut their own timber and firewood, sell their own corn, and pasture their cattle on the town moor. On the other hand the Bishop claimed dues from all fish landed and sold, and his nominee was to preside over the borough court and administer justice.

One might expect, as presumably the Bishop did, that so privileged a community would develop prosperously and speedily. In fact Wearmouth progressed little during the Middle Ages. The villagers around St Michael's Church remained concerned solely with farming matters, while the port never flourished. On the north shore the monks of St Peter's owned and rented out a wooden staith for the trans-shipment of coal brought down the river during the fourteenth century. Fishing boats and occasional small merchant vessels made their way into the river and into the little inlet at Hendon, to the south. Wine for the Bishop's household was landed, and salt, evaporated from seawater in broad shallow basins on the shore, was shipped along the coast. There were traps ('yares') in the river for salmon, but some of these interfered so much with the slowly growing traffic in coal coming down from the pits at places like Lambton and Harraton, Fatfield and Biddick, that most were removed by order of the Bishop in the fifteenth century. Enterprising local landowners like Thomas Menvil, younger son of a prominent Horden family, found it worthwhile to rent the borough with its income from tolls, fines and salmon yares; and according to one interpretation of the records Menvil also held the right to build ships (they are unlikely to have been much larger than fishing boats) in Hendon Bay. But despite these signs of activity Sunderland remained no more than an insignificant village with a population of a few score, while Newcastle was becoming a prosperous town on the strength of its coastwise and overseas trade.

The reasons for this lack of success are many. To some extent the whole North-East suffered from the constant threat of Scottish depredations, particularly after the disaster at Bannockburn in 1314. Such trade as did grow, in wool and coal, was almost entirely captured by Newcastle with its enterprising merchant guilds, regular trading links with London and the continent, and safe defensive walls. The Bishops acquired control of Hartlepool, Stockton and Gateshead, finding them in many ways more promising as ports. Wearmouth harbour remained unsatisfactory; and the Wear itself, unnavigable even by small boats beyond the 'new bridge' at Chester, failed to provide an adequate link with the interior. Finally, Wearmouth seems to have been hit especially hard by the onslaught of the Black Death in 1349.

When Bishop Hatfield, shortly before his death in 1381, ordered a new survey of his lands, it revealed no very fundamental changes at the river mouth in the two hundred years since Boldon Book. Sunderland, the borough held by Thomas Menvil, is clearly distinguished from Wearmouth. In the latter there was some evidence of social and economic progress; the Bishop's tenants were more varied in their status and in the extent of the lands that each held scattered through the open fields and moors. They paid the bulk of their dues to the Bishop in money rather than in kind or in labour services, rendering, for example, six shillings each St Martin's Day instead of one milch cow, and ten shillings on St Cuthbert's Day for 'cornage'.

It is perhaps difficult to envisage the three medieval villages clustered about the river mouth. The cottages on Monkwearmouth shore were dominated by the tall old tower of St Peter's. The fisherfolk, and the peasants settled round the village green a quarter of a mile inland (near the later 'Wheatsheaf'), paid their dues and looked for justice and guidance to the Prior of the Benedictines at Durham, attending thrice yearly at his Halmote Court for the settlement of their disputes and the regulation of their affairs. The cottages of Bishopwearmouth were spaced around its rectangular green; it too was dominated by the stone-built church and the rectory, their materials quarried from Building Hill, which all villagers could claim to use freely. Its great open fields and moors stretched as far as Ryhope, and its parochial jurisdiction was one of the largest in Durham. Its villagers took their problems to the Bishop's Halmote Court, held by his officers at Houghton-le-Spring, for administratively Bishopwearmouth was but one vill of a substantial manor. Sunderland straggled along the river bank. The future Low Street, just above the shore line, and High Street, running up towards Bishopwearmouth and known as 'the royal street', already existed. South from the royal street stretched the burgage plots, the ridges or rigs of farming land that were the private property of the burgesses and on which they built their houses. Their shape became fossilized into the pattern of long, narrow streets that led off High Street until (and even after) the great rebuilding of the nineteenth century. Beyond, to the south, lay the Lord Bishop's Moor, the Town Moor as it was later to become, on which the burgesses had the right to pasture their animals, bleach their cloth, or dry their nets.

When, with the Tudors, a new age seemed to be dawning in England, it was slow to affect Wearmouth. The three communities remained much as they had been throughout the Middle Ages, save that soon after 1536 the last monks left St Peter's and their property passed to a lay owner. As late as 1565 a commission set up by Queen Elizabeth described only a sleepy coastal village: 'A fishing town and landing place called Sunderland which has 30 householders ... but there are neither ships nor boats and only 7 cobles that belong to the town, occupying 20 fishermen. The town is in great decay of building and inhabitants...'

But the years of change and growth were at hand.

CHAPTER FOUR

THE GROWING PORT

IN the last years of Queen Elizabeth's reign a new era opened for Sunderland, as for the North-East in general. For centuries, and more particularly since the Reformation, the far northern counties had lagged behind the more prosperous and secure south, where men so speedily adapted themselves to continental fashions, whether in clothes, technology, economic change, religious beliefs, or the structure of society. The Roman Catholic faith and the feudal power of the nobility both remained formidable in the Border counties long after progressives in far-off London had set their faces against them. In 1569 the last medieval rising of the Catholic northern nobility was suppressed. An impoverished, troublesome backwater: such was the sophisticated Londoner's view of the far North.

Twice in its history the North-East has stepped into the forefront of human progress. It did so during that Northumbrian golden age in which Wearmouth monastery played so important a part. It took a leading role again during the centuries of the Industrial Revolution, when the mineral wealth of the Pennine flanks helped win Britain its place as the world's richest and most progressive country. As those minerals were exploited, so the ports exporting them flourished and grew.

Coal had been mined and exported from County Durham for centuries. Newcastle had largely built its prosperity upon its domination of this trade, and its powerful Company of Hostmen (that is, those who held the right to act as 'host' to visiting merchants, supervising their purchases) claimed a monopoly of the valuable commerce with London. Small quantities of coal had long come down the Wear, and in the fifteenth century the monks of St Peter's had leased their staith to such enterprising landowners as William Lambton, already building the fortune and estates that were to place his descendants among the foremost families of the North. But Newcastle's dominance, strengthened by the bargain of 1600 when the Queen recognized the monopoly in return for a tax of a shilling a chaldron on Tyne coals, long held back the growth of other ports.

However, the demand for new fuel supplies in the growing towns was rising urgently. Britain's forests were threatened with exhaustion as more and more timber went into ships and houses. Coal was being put to a host of new uses in order to fill the gap.

In 1589 Robert Bowes of Barnes leased a strip of land on the south bank of the river, just above the fishing village. He was a distinguished member of a family that had long been prominent in County Durham and whose members had frequently held the borough of Sunderland, with all its rights and dues, over the past 130 years. Robert Bowes had followed a varied career in diplomacy and administration, and now in his old age he chose to invest in a new enterprise. His partner was a King's Lynn merchant. Prosperous shipowners of the East Anglian ports dominated much of the east coast trade; theirs were the ships that carried most of the coal from the

The Growing Port

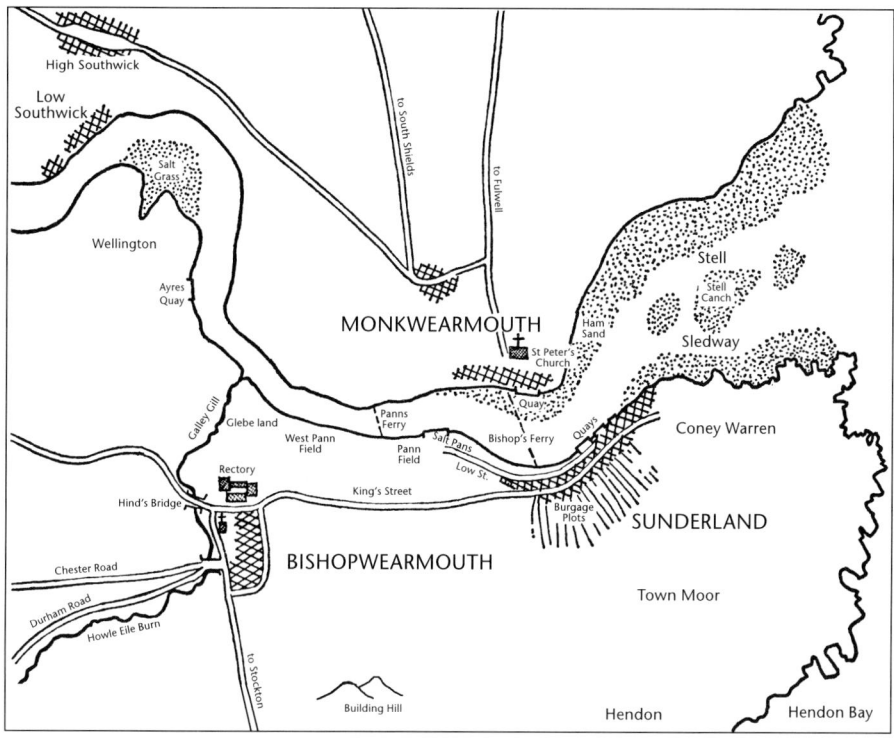

The settlements at the mouth of the Wear in the seventeenth century

Tyne and they were the merchants who most resented the Hostmen's monopoly. Such men were ready and able to sink capital into the industry of an impoverished region with a promising future.

The new venture that Robert Bowes and John Smith planned for their riverside land was centred on the developing salt industry. Whereas in the past salt had been produced by evaporation, mainly along the south and east coasts, or imported from Brittany, now it was to be boiled in great iron pans. These were twenty feet and more square, and five or six feet deep; and beneath them a furnace was kept blazing for three and a half days at white heat, boiling the pan dry over and over again. On his strip of land, which soon came to be known as the 'Panns', Bowes set up ten of these, housed in wooden sheds that also held stocks of coal and provided dwellings for the few workmen needed to operate the equipment. Each pan could be counted on to produce 3,200 bushels of salt in a year, but for that it needed twenty tons of coal, roughly six tons of it to produce each ton of salt. By the 1630s some 50,000 bushels of salt were being produced annually on the banks of the Wear.

The coal for Bowes' pans came down the Wear from places like Lambton and Harraton, and from the new pit that he and his partner sank at Offerton. He needed only coarse, low-grade fuel for his enterprise, so was able to export the better quality coal. His organization was on a large scale, something almost unprecedented in the

North-East; he and Smith are said to have sunk £4,000 of capital altogether into their ventures, and to have employed 300 workmen. At Sunderland they built a new quay, Bowes Quay, at which to load salt and coal, and over the next few decades it was joined by other quays, George Lilburne's for example, and Robert Ayres' Quay up at Deptford, built about 1629.

Other industries soon followed Bowes' on the banks of the Wear as other entrepreneurs sought to imitate his success. All made use of the large quantities of cheap coal that were available, and of the easy transport by sea to ports throughout the kingdom. Lime was burnt in large quantities, and the remains of the stone kilns can still be seen along the river banks. It was shipped out for use as mortar or as fertilizer. Two agents essential for fixing and intensifying colours in the days before aniline dyes, copperas and alum, were soon being produced at furnaces on the river side. The key factor in each case was the nearness of the pits a little way up the river; of the other raw materials, limestone was ready to hand and the rest could easily be brought in by sea. Some of the pyrites required for copperas came, for example, from Lyme in Dorset.

To some extent all these industries were common to much of the North-East coast. The greatest centre of salt production, for example, was at South Shields, where production far overshadowed that of Sunderland; by the end of the century it was at least eight times as large. Many Sunderland developments followed a pattern already established in Newcastle; this was certainly the case with the glass manufacture that began late in the seventeenth century. Again, the supply of coal was important.

As coal-burning industries grew along the Wear, so did the export of good quality coal for domestic use in London, East Anglia, and the Low Countries. By 1609 Wearmouth was shipping out nearly 12,000 tons a year, though this was a trifle compared with Newcastle's quarter of a million tons. Sunderland's harbour was still accessible only to the smallest vessels, and there must have been by this time some two or three hundred of them using it annually. Sunderland's growth during these early decades of the seventeenth century is reflected in the coal export figures. In the twenty-five years up to 1634 they increased sixfold to 69,000 tons; in the same period Newcastle's had nearly doubled, to 453,000 tons.

In this industrial and commercial development Sunderland, though much overshadowed by its old-established and powerful neighbour, had one notable advantage. Newcastle was so completely dominated by the group of wealthy merchants belonging to the Company of Hostmen, particularly since Queen Elizabeth's charter had granted them virtually complete control of local government, that there was little opportunity for enterprising young men from outside their closed ranks. Those who wished to prosper from the new boom conditions avoided their restrictive influence by moving instead to the rising port on the Wear. The prospect of profitable rewards for enterprise and hard work is said to have attracted numbers of Scots to settle in the town; but probably more typical and certainly more noteworthy was the career of George Lilburne.

Lilburne was second son of a prominent landowning family from the Bishop Auckland area. After early attempts to establish himself in Newcastle he came to

Sunderland some time before 1620, and soon became the town's leading merchant, 'the great factotum of Sunderland that rules both the religion and wealth of the town', as a hostile clergyman described him. Soon he was running a fleet of his own ships, challenging the domination hitherto enjoyed by East Anglian vessels; and his little craft may well have been built on the banks of the Wear. Like Robert Bowes and his other predecessors he needed outside capital, and like them he drew it from cooperation with London and East Anglian merchants ready to invest in the booming North-East. Soon he and his partners were leasing collieries from the landowners higher up the river at Lumley, Lambton and Harraton. He ran a fleet of keel-boats on the river and a farm outside the town, while in it he was chandler, grocer, mercer, and linen draper. Lilburne exemplified the manifold profitable activities open to an enterprising young man in those exciting years for the North-East.

Sunderland was growing in size and importance. By the 1630s its population seems to have passed the 1,000 mark, and by 1642 there were about 1,400 inhabitants of the port alone. It was important enough by 1627 to give its name to an earl when Lord Scrope, one of Charles I's least successful public servants, took his new title from it. In 1634 Lilburne and his fellow merchants sought recognition for the town's new-found importance and confirmation of the long-dormant borough rights. Bishop Morton duly granted a new charter, reviving the old privileges in up-dated form. It provided for a mayor, together with a body of twelve aldermen, appointed for life by the charter and including George Lilburne, together with twenty-four councillors.

As first mayor the charter nominated Sir William Bellasyse, one of the Palatinate's leading gentry, High Sheriff of the county since 1625 and resident at Morton House near Houghton-le-Spring. Like so many others among his fellow landowners he was already deeply involved in the growing exploitation of, and trade in, the coal along the banks of the Wear, as well as in the prosperous salt industry of South Shields.

The corporation thus created apparently functioned for the next few years, and Lilburne, the only alderman from the port of Sunderland itself, succeeded Bellasyse as mayor and was re-elected several times. But in the stresses of the Civil War period the structure of local government in the Bishopric collapsed, for Sunderland was becoming involved in the increasing frictions that divided King Charles from many of his subjects.

Sunderland's part in the Civil War demonstrates how both local and national issues affected the development of that conflict. Many of those who, like Lilburne, were making their way upwards in the world through careful administration of small estates or the profits of trade also inclined to a zealous and forthright puritanism in religion. Lilburne and his associates stoutly resented the activities and attitudes of the Laudian rector of Bishopwearmouth, and on several occasions Lilburne himself was summoned before the Archbishop's Court of High Commission to answer for his violently anticlerical behaviour. Simultaneously they resisted what they thought of as royal encroachment in trade and taxation. They objected to King Charles's imposition of Ship Money, Lilburne again leading the protest. They feared the King's alliance with the powerful Hostmen, whose monopolistic designs he still favoured in return for levies on the coal they shipped. In this the Sunderland merchants were at one with those of Yarmouth and London, who all resented Newcastle's privileged position and any attempt by the King to share in the profits of his subjects' trade.

In March, 1640, the danger of invasion from the north once more loomed as the Scots armed and marched to demonstrate their dislike of Charles's religious policy, a dislike shared by many in Sunderland. Lilburne, together with the mayor, Richard Cotterill, was accused of subversive activities; they had in fact been encouraging the soldiers being mustered to meet the invasion to desert. Lilburne's goods were seized by order of the High Sheriff, Bellasyse, for his refusal to pay Ship Money and coat-and-conduct money. Clearly he was the ringleader of a group that was very actively opposed to royal policies.

When Civil War finally broke out in 1642 Sunderland was occupied by the King's forces, and troublemakers such as Lilburne suffered indignity and imprisonment. Inevitably the port's growing trade suffered a momentary setback; in particular the coal trade was disrupted, for its market in Parliament-held London was no longer accessible and ships of the Parliament-controlled fleet blockaded the coast. The King's control of the North was for the time being complete, and since it threatened their livelihood as well as their faith the merchants of Sunderland resented it. On the other hand the plain farmers of the town were, as a group, much more inclined to sympathize with the King and to offer help in goods and service. In due course, when the war was lost, seven of them were penalized for their mistaken loyalty and paid heavy fines.

The royal domination of the North was soon broken, and Sunderland was swept briefly into the midst of the fighting that destroyed it. Parliament, with one eye on the need to secure London's coal supply, came to an agreement with the Scots, hitherto watchfully neutral. They were to join the war against the King, sending a massive army to overrun the Royalist North, and Parliament would foot their bill. Late in 1643 the formidable Scottish army, commanded by the veteran Lord Leven, gathered and advanced to occupy the town of Berwick.

In January the Scots crossed the Tweed and marched south through Northumberland, as they had marched so often before. It was hardly a good time for campaigning. Rain, mud, snow and flooded rivers hampered progress, but the Scots were borne up by their religious fervour. They came not, on this occasion, in their habitual role as raiders and robbers but as friends and brothers to spread the enlightened faith of Calvin and Knox, to destroy Papists and idolaters. They came, too, in formidable strength, some 18,000 foot and over 3,000 horse, with sixty guns. Further, they were able, since Parliament controlled the seas, to supply their army through such ports as they could capture.

The Scots reached Newcastle on 3rd February, but had little success there since the mayor and garrison resisted vigorously; their royalism was unquestioned. After some three weeks Leven found his army dispirited by lack of success, shortage of supplies, dismal weather, and a widespread, unexpected hostility from local folk who failed to appreciate good intentions and puritanical zeal, and who knew Scottish habits too well of old. He left a small force to keep an eye on Newcastle and set off on a difficult and dangerous encircling march, only practicable if he could be certain

The Growing Port

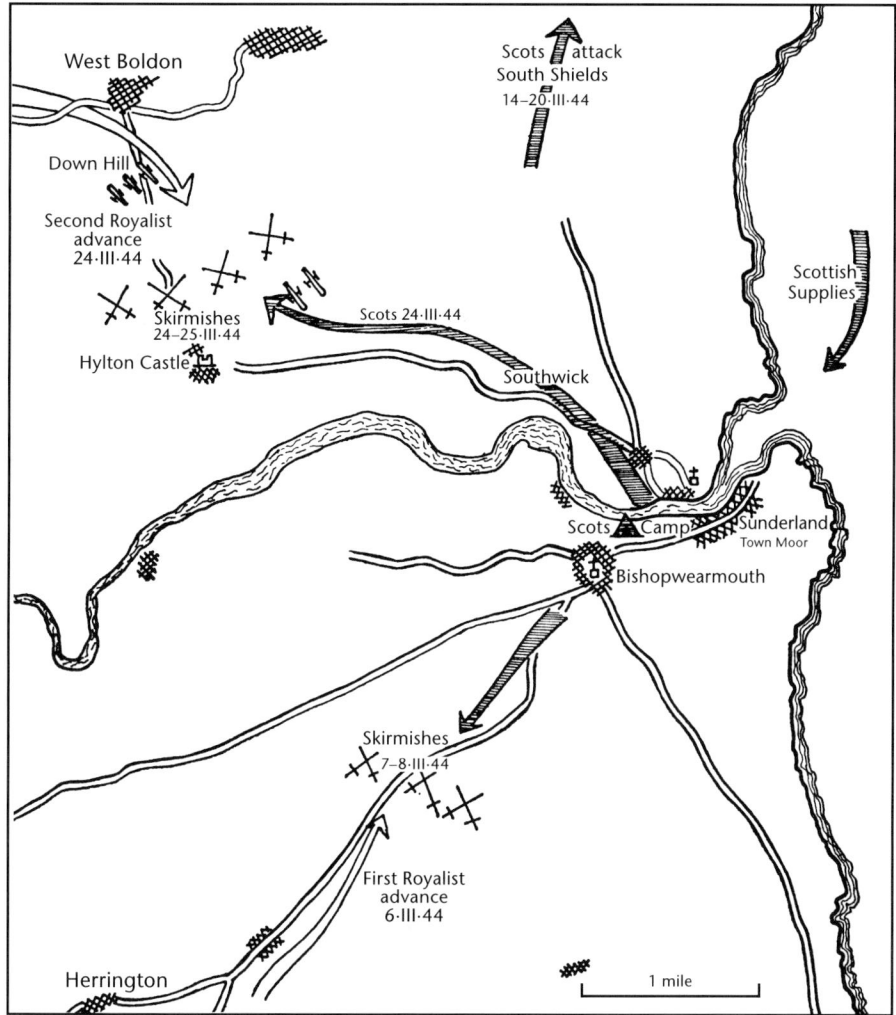

The Civil War clashes

of a secure haven on the coast and sea-borne supplies. At the end of February the Scots crossed the Tyne, unhindered by the hovering Royalist cavalry. They pushed on across the Derwent and the Wear, observed and occasionally harried as they drove eastwards for the sea. They were much too strong for the dilatory Marquis of Newcastle, the King's commander in the North, to risk an attack, and he was urgently summoning reinforcements from Yorkshire.

Leven's army made its way to Herrington, within sight of the sea at last, by 2nd March; and there they rested for the Sunday, the Lord's Day. Any Royalist troops still in Bishopwearmouth hastily withdrew across the river, and on the 4th the Scots entered unopposed and presumably welcomed by some at least of the townspeople.

Building a formidably entrenched encampment in West Panns field, a strong position on high ground overlooking the river, they prepared to receive supplies and resist attack.

The Scottish position was not an easy one. They badly needed supplies but the local people offered little; save among some of the merchants and seamen there was suspicion and hostility. Bad weather hampered supplies from Scotland; three ships had been lost at sea on the way and two others, driven into the Tyne, were captured by Royalists. But two cargoes of good Scottish oatmeal did at last get through, and another vessel arrived with cheese and butter from London.

Meanwhile the Royalists, now reinforced, made a threatening gesture and appeared on the 6th on high ground two or three miles to the south-west. There they stayed throughout the next day, which was bleak and snowy, in a strong position. Neither side dared risk an attack, although there was skirmishing among the lanes and hedges between small parties of musketeers and horsemen. The Royalists, camped in the open fields in a bitter wind, suffered seriously from exposure, numbers of men and horses died or deserted, and early on the 8th they withdrew hurriedly after firing some villages, their cavalry holding off Scottish attempts to harry them.

With this threat removed, the Scots settled into their camp and rested. On the 13th they began a move towards Durham, but this was perhaps a feint for they had apparently decided to strengthen their base on the coast before advancing towards the main Royalist forces. They returned, crossed the Wear, and attacked the fort commanding the entry to the Tyne at South Shields. The defenders, only 100 strong but supported from across the river by the heavy guns of Tynemouth Castle and by a Royalist ship at anchor off shore, beat them off. A second assault a few days later was more successful, and the Scots also captured a number of vessels carrying coal and salt that lay in the Tyne.

Still short of forage for his horses, Leven hesitated over his next move until a fresh Royalist threat developed. The Marquis of Newcastle on 23rd March moved through Chester-le-Street and on the 24th occupied Boldon Hill and the high ground north of Hylton Castle. The Scots hastily brought their main force across from their camp to face him, despite the fact that the Marquis had unfairly chosen the Lord's Day for his advance. As dusk drew on the Royalist cannon began to bombard the assembling Scots. With the aid of Sunderland keelmen and fisherfolk the Scots were able to get one of their own big guns over the river, apparently losing another in the process which was, three centuries later, salvaged to stand in Barnes Park.

The Marquis showed his habitual caution. Having failed to catch a part of the Scottish force away from their camp, and finding the ground too broken by hedges and ditches to allow a successful attack, he contented himself once more with small-scale skirmishing; and having lost the initiative he decided there was nothing for it but to withdraw again. Next morning, after attempting to deceive the Scots by marching his men about on the hill and throwing up new breastworks for his cannon, he fell back hurriedly, leaving the cavalry as usual to beat off, with considerable success, an attempt by the Scottish horse to attack his rear.

Sunderland was secured for Parliament, and with it as a base for their supplies

The Growing Port

The Scottish cannon, lost in the Wear in 1644, that stands now in Barnes Park

the Scots marched off on the road to Easington, Durham and ultimately to the last great confrontation at Marston Moor. The Sunderland seamen themselves seem to have been largely responsible for keeping the town in Parliamentary hands when, a few weeks later, South Shields was betrayed to the King. Soon they were aided by reinforcements from Parliament, and then fresh Scottish forces arrived to capture Hartlepool, Stockton and Gateshead, making their grip on the whole county secure.

Briefly, between March and the fall of Newcastle in October, Sunderland served as a Parliamentary naval base. The Earl of Warwick's ships, operating from the town, took four Royalist vessels in March, and in July a captured arms vessel with twenty-two cannon for the King's forces was brought into the harbour. Sunderland's coal trade flourished that summer as it supplied London's needs without competition from Newcastle, still in Royalist hands; but the collier fleet remained subject to the danger of attack from Royalist ships operating out of Scarborough, and no less than forty loaded vessels were reported fallen into enemy hands in October.

Sunderland and the rest of the county remained firmly under the control of Parliament, represented by commissioners headed by Sir William Armyne, who were for a time based in Sunderland. Now the Lilburnes and their friends at last came into their own. George Lilburne remained the most prominent figure in the town throughout the period of the Commonwealth, while his nephew Robert, a colonel in the Parliamentary army, became one of the leading men in the county.

Another nephew, the famous radical pamphleteer known as 'Free-born John', soon fell out with Cromwell's repressive regime.

But the destruction of the old regime in the borough and the Bishopric did not bring tranquillity, and there was a series of conflicts over confiscated royalist lands and political power. George Lilburne and his nephews clashed in the courts time and again with other ambitious landowners who sought to profit from the wholesale disposal of estates and mines.

One result of the war was the virtual destruction of Newcastle's monopolistic ambitions, which aided the further development of Sunderland. Despite the fact that the Newcastle merchants jealously tried, over the next century and more, to hamper the growth of their neighbour's trade, Sunderland's coal exports rose steadily. By the end of the seventeenth century Sunderland was shipping out something like a quarter of a million tons annually, more than a third of Newcastle's total. Other industries also flourished, and enterprising manufacturers found Wearside a good place to set up in business. One such, who came to Sunderland primarily for its advantages of position rather than because of the abundance of coal, was Ambrose Crowley, who set up his iron manufactory off Low Street in 1682. He explained to the ironmasters of the Midlands with whom he had formerly traded that at Sunderland he could easily bring in iron from Sweden or from anywhere on the English coast, frequently without cost since it was carried by collier vessels returning in ballast. Similarly he could export his products far more easily than the land-bound Birmingham manufacturers. But Crowley did not remain long in Sunderland; finding local hostility to his foreign workmen he moved about 1690 to Winlaton, near the Tyne.

The fast-growing commercial traffic raised the problem of the inadequacy of the river as a harbour. The difficulty was twofold. The river mouth tended to become obstructed by sandbanks and shoals; outside there was the dangerous bar, where shallow and broken water led to many a wreck as vessels tried beating into the river before a north-easterly gale. To the north and south of this were ominous stretches of flat rock. And once past these outer hazards ships had to make their way by narrow, shifting channels on one side or the other of the broad sandbank known as the Stell Canch. Ships coming in to load coal soon added to these obstructions by depositing their ballast of sand, gravel or mud indiscriminately as they entered harbour or as they lay at anchor; and even when ballast was dumped ashore on the flat ground below St Peter's Church, it was frequently washed down by the tide.

But once safely anchored a fresh problem faced ships' masters. The river banks were either of crumbling mud and gravel, or backed by difficult limestone cliffs. It was only possible to load or unload cargo at certain states of the tide, and the constant passage of heavily laden keelmen and sailors, coal waggons and carriers tended to break down the banks. Much loading was done in the river, direct from keel boat to collier; but save where substantial stone quays had been built the banks nevertheless suffered heavily.

These problems were at first the concern of the Bishop's Water Bailiff, and in the seventeenth century were partly transferred to a body of local worthies known as Commissioners of Sewers, who were authorized to check the dumping of ballast and

The Growing Port

rubbish, and to conserve the banks. Meanwhile enterprising merchants continued, like Lilburne and Robert Ayres, to build their own deep-water quays.

In 1669 royal letters patent granted Edward Andrews power to erect piers, provide lighthouses and prohibit the depositing of ballast, levying a tonnage duty on ships using the port in return; but little in fact seems to have been done. Spasmodic attempts continued to authorize cleansing and clearing of the river, and disputes were frequent among those who held property on the banks or claimed rights over the mudflats. There seems to have been some improvement, and an increase in the size of vessels that could use the harbour; whereas early in the century the average cargo of coal was twenty-five tons, by its end it had reached sixty tons. At the same time the average cargo leaving the Tyne was more like 250 tons. Newcastle Hostmen were contemptuous of their small rival: 'It is dangerous in winter both for the ships to lye in the roads there and for the keels to go out to them,' said one complacently in 1705. 'There is no safety,' wrote 'J.C.' in *The Compleat Collier* of 1708, 'there wants a Peor, ... besides the Bar is so choaked up that there is great want of Water.' Newcastle men recognized, however, that were it not for these disadvantages, Sunderland merchants might well challenge their domination, for the Wear was best part of a day's sailing nearer London. They resisted, strongly and successfully, a move of 1706 to get parliamentary sanction for major improvements to Sunderland harbour.

Eventually, in 1717, the Wear coalowners and merchants, appalled by the cluttered river and consequent delays to shipping, combined to promote another improvement bill; they wanted a body with statutory powers to ensure that the river was kept properly navigable as far as the staiths at Fatfield. They found themselves still opposed by the Newcastle interests, but this time their bill was duly passed and the River Wear Commissioners came into existence. The Commissioners acted with common sense and some vigour, and throughout the eighteenth century they were generally successful in keeping adequate harbour facilities open. They made, and sometimes enforced, regulations against ballast dumping and quay building, they surveyed the river bed and its difficulties in detail, and they levied the dues to which they were entitled on the shipping using the facilities they provided. The general effect was to secure the banks, narrow the channel, and clear its bottom. About 1723 they began the building of the South Pier, to control and direct the flow of the river. In 1752 their engineer set to work to open up the southern channel, the Sledway, past the Stell Canch, closing the northern one by means of driving piles and sinking old keels, making a more or less permanent alteration to the geography of the river.

The result was a period of steady growth in trade and shipping. By the 1740s Sunderland was exporting some 330,000 tons of coal annually, nearly half of Newcastle's total; and by the 1770s, at over 600,000 tons, it was two-thirds of Newcastle's. The bulk of the coal was still carried in vessels owned in Yarmouth, Lynn or London, but ships from North-East ports, Whitby, Scarborough, Newcastle and Sunderland itself, were increasingly playing a part. By 1752 190 ships belonged to Sunderland, and this had increased to 350 by 1776. In 1752, 3,597 ships in all used the port, and their average size was growing steadily, to 300 or 400 tons by mid-century. At the same time the number of keels on the river, plying up and down to the staiths, increased in proportion, and by 1799 there were 520 of them, more than on the Tyne.

Behind this expanding commerce a host of other industries grew. Ships of increasing size and number were being built; shipbuilders are recorded in the town with increasing frequency from the middle of the seventeenth century on. There were the Goodchilds of Pallion who, from about 1672, were building small vessels averaging 70 to 80 tons for transporting the lime produced by their kilns: and there were the Burns who, from 1691, were building ships on Monkwearmouth shore, at Hylton, or at Deptford. They were among a host of unrecorded others in the days when building a little wooden vessel on a stretch of open river bank was a straightforward enterprise for any family with the necessary skills and a little capital; and in most of these cases the shipbuilding activities grew out of the need to transport the products of a family industry.

Shipbuilding spawned its own ancillary industries, notably sailmaking and rope manufacture, and in the eighteenth century the long 'walks' where ropes were plaited at their full length stretched across the Town Moor or alongside the streets. Other industries continued to add new smoking chimneys to the many that now dotted the river bank. A new copperas works was opened in Deptford in 1772, and that district soon became a thriving industrial suburb. From about mid-century the manufacture of pottery became increasingly important; again raw materials were imported cheaply as ballast, fuel was readily available, and the sea provided a relatively easy route to markets in London or the continent. The earliest potteries in the district were at Newbottle and Silksworth; by 1762 they were on the Wear at North Hylton, and at least four potteries were working in the Wearmouth area by the end of the century.

Economically, the Wear had come to vigorous life, and as its commerce and industry grew so country folk moved in to the prospering town at its mouth, and the houses and streets began their advance into the green fields about it.

Chapter Five

One Town

As commerce and industry flourished around the mouth of the Wear, so the three settlements expanded. Their joint population probably amounted to over 5,000 by the end of the seventeenth century, and by that time Sunderland had far more inhabitants than its neighbours. When the people of the port petitioned in 1712 to be created a separate parish they claimed to number 6,000 souls. Ninety years later, when the first census was taken, there were 24,000 people living in the three communities.

The rapid growth of the late seventeenth and eighteenth centuries particularly affected Sunderland itself, and increasingly it became an area of crowded, narrow streets and tall, jumbled houses two and three storeys high. Wealthy merchants erected stately stone mansions, or used the new-fangled bricks, for which suitable clay could be dug on the Bishop's Moor despite the occasional protests of the Bishop. The town houses of local landowning families like the Lambtons in High Street, and the fashionable new developments like Church Street overlooked the tangle of meaner dwellings, pierced only by narrow alleys and stairs and closes that lay between High Street and the river. Enterprising folk sought to carve out for themselves tracts of the Town Moor, as the Bishop's Moor was now generally known; and the occupation of this land gave rise to many a legal dispute among the 'freemen and stallingers', who claimed rights to it dating back to Bishop Morton's charter and beyond, and between these claimants and the Bishop, who held that their rights covered pasturage alone.

On the Intake land carved from the Moor a fine new church was built, dedicated in the momentous year 1719 when Sunderland finally won parochial independence. The ancient and extensive parish of Bishopwearmouth was split up; the people of the port no longer plodded each Sunday along the uphill mile of High Street. The new parish was a compact area, hemmed in by river and sea, limited on the south by the Town Moor and the lane that later became Coronation Street, and on the west by the line that was to be Sans Street.

The new parish church of Holy Trinity reflected in its fabric and interior the newly prosperous community that had built it. Externally it was unexciting, in serviceable red brick. In its simple classical architecture the splendours of the age of Wren were modified by the purposeful seriousness of northern merchants. The interior, perhaps the most impressive of Sunderland's well-hidden delights, reveals the life and faith of those who subscribed for it, rejecting the gloomy grey Gothic of St Michael's. It was light and airy, with seven pairs of very large and plain windows. It was straightforward, reflecting the eighteenth century's preference for sermons and reason in place of mystery and ritual; it had a box-like nave and a gallery (soon there were others in the aisles) to accommodate the port's teaming people, a plain pulpit and no chancel to accommodate the rector; though in 1735 a rector with views and

The light and elegant interior of Sunderland parish church

money of his own added a small, nearly circular apse. Slender columns in the Corinthian manner supported gallery and roof. Proudly and prominently the royal arms and those of two lordly bishops were displayed, demonstrating where the parishioners' loyalty lay in an age when the authority of kings and churchmen was facing challenge. Substantial stalls were provided for the important officials of local government, labelled with their titles: constable, overseer, churchwarden. Finally, a sizeable vestry room was incorporated, attached not to the rector's chancel but to the parishioners' nave, for this was to be the meeting place of those principally responsible for administering the new parish, and in the eighteenth century the parish was the basic unit of local government. In the vestry the twenty-four gentlemen of Sunderland, elected by their fellow ratepayers, and meeting under the chairmanship of the rector, dealt with the knotty problems of a crowded, busy town. They had to keep the streets clean, well-drained and surfaced, to provide for the poor and the sick, to guard against such hazards as fire. They assessed and collected church rates and poor rates. They built (about 1740) a workhouse in Church Lane, paid for by public subscription and holding, at one time, as many as 600 people. They provided a charity school in the churchyard. And they paid or supervised a group of busy officials, the overseers of the poor, the churchwardens with their many functions, the constables (eventually there were twenty-eight), even the rector himself.

Sunderland, with its fine new church and large houses, overshadowed its older neighbours. Bishopwearmouth remained a relatively sleepy country town. Its cottages and houses had been largely rebuilt in the limestone quarried from Building Hill. About it the open fields and the two moors, north and south, had been partitioned among the freeholders since 1649. It was growing, though much more slowly than the port, as industry and commerce spread along the river bank and on into Deptford which, by the end of the century was becoming an industrial suburb, with bottle works, shipyards, copperas works and ropery. Traffic and travellers going to and from Sunderland usually passed through the older centre before taking one of the roads that radiated from it, to Chester-le-Street, Durham or Stockton. As with Sunderland the local administration was (at least from 1661, when the last vestiges of Bishop Morton's borough disappeared) in the hands of the vestry; and the vestry was dominated by the rector, by far the most important figure in Bishopwearmouth, whose fine house with extensive grounds, outbuildings and tithe barn occupied the northern end of the town. Beyond the rectory and overlooking the river a rectangular grid of streets was laid out in the last decade of the century as Bishopwearmouth grew towards its flourishing neighbour.

Monkwearmouth and Monkwearmouth Shore remained relatively small, though they too grew as the shipyards multiplied. The townships were dominated, from the late seventeenth century on, by the Williamson family, whose Jacobean manor house lay opposite the old church. Up river the former hamlets of North and

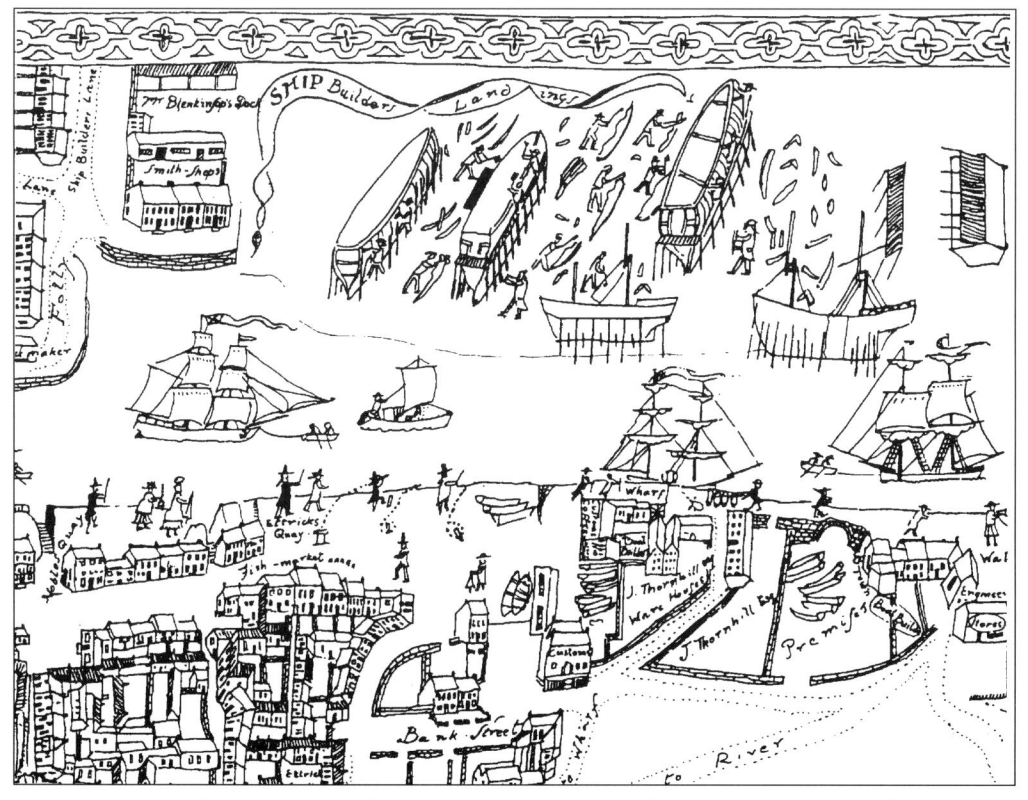

A fascinating depiction of Wearside in the 1780s by John Rain, who portrays shipbuilding occurring at Monkwearmouth Shore, opposite part of Sunderland's 'east end'

South Hylton and Southwick all grew and prospered as they too benefited from the activity on the Wear, developing their own potteries, shipyards and glassworks.

By the end of the eighteenth century 12,000 people were crowded into the compact area of Sunderland, compared with Bishopwearmouth's relatively widespread 6,000 and the 5,000 who lived on the northern side of the river. But Sunderland itself no longer held the houses of the gentry or wealthy merchants. Those who could afford it moved into elegant mansions scattered through the fields between the port and Bishopwearmouth, or beyond the latter out in the open country to the west and south; older houses like High and Low Barnes and Bainbridge Holme, newer ones like Ford Hall, Thornhill, the Grange, Building Hill or Hendon House. None of these survive now save as district names. Many other folk, less opulent, chose to live in the more spacious houses of Bishopwearmouth or Southwick, so that those who profited from the busy activity of the port enjoyed their wealth in the neighbouring parish. By 1823 Bishopwearmouth, with less than two-thirds of Sunderland's population, was worth three times as much in rateable value; and as Bishopwearmouth donned an air of satisfied prosperity so Sunderland seemed ever more crowded, dirty and slummy. The commissioners who, in 1836, investigated the town's claim to borough status, described it as 'with the exception of one street, where there are some respectable houses and shops, one mass of small houses crowded together, with interstices of narrow lanes rather than streets'.

Physical growth was inevitably drawing the three separate communities together as ribbon development spread along both the river banks, with their warehouses, workshops and crowded houses, and along the High Street with its more substantial buildings. The more isolated community that faced Sunderland on the northern shore had long been in contact with it by ferry. Until the clearing activities of the Wear Commissioners it had been possible to cross the river mouth on foot at low tide; but the drier, safer and more usual passage since the Middle Ages had been by way of the Bishop's Ferry, from Low Quay at the foot of Bodlewell Lane. There were several alternative ferries; the Panns Ferry, a little higher up the river and just below the present bridge, was mainly for horses and cattle; and there were others beyond it, at Deptford and Hylton. But as the towns grew the need for easier intercommunication became urgent. In 1796 it was at last provided with the building of that wonder of its age, the iron bridge.

The bridge was sponsored by Rowland Burdon of Castle Eden, landowner, shrewd business man, twice Mayor of Stockton, and Member of Parliament. He was already deeply involved in the improvement and turnpiking that linked Wearmouth more efficiently to Stockton and the south. In 1792 he obtained an Act of Parliament authorising the appointment of commissioners to raise money and plan the bridging of the river at Sunderland.

But bridging the Wear presented many problems. There could be no question of interrupting the busy traffic that flowed unceasingly along what was now a major highway. At Newcastle, of course, the bridge was old established; port, shipyards, most of the riverside industry had all developed immediately *below* the point at which it blocked the river to shipping. But at Sunderland no similar obstruction would be acceptable; the bridge must be high above the river, linking the cliffs rather than the narrow banks below them; and those cliffs, at their nearest, were some 240 feet apart.

This was a formidable span for eighteenth century technology. True there was a fine stone bridge of over 100 foot span not so far away in the famous Causey Arch, but that carried only a colliery waggonway running from Tanfield Pit down towards the Tyne, not the busy traffic that would need to cover twice that distance across the Wear. So Rowland Burdon and his associates proposed to solve the problem by revolutionary methods: they would use iron in place of conventional wood or stone.

There was already one famous iron bridge, built by Abraham Darby and spanning the Severn at Coalbrookdale. It was a comparatively modest affair, a mere 100 feet across and only forty feet above the water at its centre. Such dimensions would not serve for the Wear, and Burdon, with the building contractor, the experienced Thomas Wilson of Bishopwearmouth, needed something altogether more spectacular. They made use of plans devised by the famous radical, Tom Paine, for a bridge to be built in America. Their scheme involved hollow blocks of cast iron, four inches thick, which were substituted for the stones of a more traditional bridge, giving it lightness combined with firmness. One hundred and five of these iron blocks, held together by bars of wrought iron bolted into grooves in their sides, were fitted into each of six curving ribs; on these iron ribs rested a wooden framework and lead roof, and on this was the roadway, thirty-two feet wide. The immense task was carried out with speed and efficiency, interrupting river traffic only very briefly; once the tall stone abutments had been completed it took only ten days to build the graceful arches linking them, and then it was a simple matter of laying the roadway while busy colliers plied below.

Reconstructed and enlarged by Robert Stephenson in 1858–9, Sunderland Bridge remained until its replacement in 1928 the largest single-arch cast iron bridge in the country. 'Hail Burdon in his Iron Boots, who strides from shore to shore,' sang the ballad-makers of the day. A hundred feet above low water and 236 feet long, it was Sunderland's most notable landmark and proudest possession, commemorated in the transfer-printed views that decorated a million pieces of local pottery. It was opened on August 9th, 1796, amid great celebrations, pomp and ceremony, and only after a force of 1,000 men from militia regiments stationed in the town had fearlessly marched across to test it.

The bridge welded together the three communities of the river mouth into one. Not only did it link the two sides of the Wear, but since its southern end lay midway between Sunderland and Bishopwearmouth it led to the development of a new commercial and social nucleus in the area separating the two older settlements. The original axis of settlement, running east-west along the river and parallel with it as traffic moved between Bishopwearmouth and the port, was overlaid by a new line running from north to south. Traffic poured along this new line, despite the bridge tolls that were paid until 1885, and now direct roads out of the town to north and south speedily developed. Sizeable houses, taverns and chapels soon filled North Bridge Street; and south of the bridge estates of fine residential streets were developed during the 1820s and '30s by landowners and builders, notably the Fawcett family. Here, in Fawcett Street, John Street, Frederick Street and Foyle

Foyle Street, built to house members of Sunderland's middle class

Street lived those moderately prosperous middle class and professional people who could no longer tolerate the overcrowded squalor of Sunderland. By the 1830s this was regarded as the best residential area of the town, orderly terraces of brick and limestone with porticoed and pillared doorways, fronted by iron railings and flights of steps. The occasional church or Wesleyan chapel contributed dignity and variety, and the newest social and cultural centre for the gentry, the Athenaeum, graced the southern end of Fawcett Street.

The move southwards from the new focus of the town extended beyond this estate. By the 1840s and '50s the best people lived in large isolated houses scattered spaciously along the line of Ryhope Road; Bede Tower, Nicholson (later Carlton) House, Ashburne House, South Moor had all been added or rebuilt during the first half of the century. Then in the 1850s Burdon Road was cut through Building Hill to extend the Fawcett Street axis in a direct link with Ryhope Road and the main road to Stockton. Within a decade or two the middle class had followed the wealthy, building such mid-century terraces as Grange Crescent, the Esplanade, and the Cloisters, and such closed-off private roads as Park Place and the Oaks. Two decades later it was the turn of the working class, leapfrogging past to occupy the rectangular grids of cottage housing further south still, between Ryhope Road and the industrialised coastline of Hendon.

The social and cultural centre of unified Sunderland became, in the first half of the nineteenth century, this newly developing segment stretching southwards from the new bridge. Meanwhile the older areas deteriorated. Bishopwearmouth developed its own crowded working-class streets near the river or along the line of Chester Road and Hylton Road and into Deptford. Many of the remaining good stone houses around the old green were split up into tenements. In mid-century the rector departed from his spacious rectory, one of the finest lesser houses in the North, where it was said that he had been better housed than any other rector in England and most bishops. He moved instead to a roomy brick mansion in Gray Road, newly developed off the fashionable Ryhope Road. He took with him the stately staircase, but the rest of the fine old rectory was ruthlessly demolished to be replaced by mean streets.

Sunderland was in a far worse plight. All the large houses left in High Street, Church Street, or the other formerly fashionable areas were split into tenements or used as warehouses, factories, workshops, taverns. In the busy human anthill there were blacksmiths, anchor-smiths, mastmakers and blockmakers, coopers, ironfounders, chainmakers' workshops and sailmakers' lofts. Sailors and shipwrights and coal-heavers now thronged the former homes of prosperous merchants, and to cater for them the public houses, the brothels, the seamen's missions, multiplied alongside one another. Breweries, smithies, a covered market jostled with the overcrowded and waterless tenements along narrow cobbled lanes and dark covered entries to produce in Sunderland conditions similar to those in many another contemporary boom town where growth had outrun the provision of public amenities and services, particularly those that dealt with the enormous, foul waste product of such a human and industrial mass. Houses in the parish held on average nine or ten inhabitants, and less than 7% of them had privies of their own. Sunless courts hidden behind shabby, crumbling facades were packed with coal bunkers, stagnating water tanks, middens and privies, fostering foul smells and ill-health. The one broad street, High Street itself, was crowded with market stalls; corn, poultry, butcher's meat, fruit, earthenware, and for a time, cattle, each had their own market area in the street. Piggeries abounded, and dunghills were carefully preserved against the visits of the parish scavenger, to be sold profitably as ripe manure for farmers. The most notorious of the slums was the Hat Case, off Fitters Row, which had been built a century before to provide elegant homes for coal agents, shipmasters and keelmen. Now, in 1845, it was described as dominated by a dunghill that was 'the chief depository for all the abomination of the neighbourhood, and one which is cried out against as a great public nuisance. The privies of the factory houses empty into ... this row, in which human ordure and other disgusting objects are so thickly deposited that one can hardly step clear of them.'

One consequence of these primitive and overcrowded conditions was the quick spread of Asiatic Cholera when that dreaded disease arrived at Sunderland in 1831, striking almost exclusively in the dismal east end. The epidemic had spread from Russia, arriving with ample warning in mid-October. The town's doctors formed themselves into a committee to fight it, led by the formidable Ulsterman William Reid Clanny, long a prominent resident of more than local fame. But shipowners and merchants were inclined to pour cold water on the alarmism of some medical men. Fearing a quarantine and consequent loss of business in the port they met publicly to express their doubts, suggesting that there was in fact no cholera in the town but only the fever normally endemic in the slum districts. The medical experts were soon arguing amongst themselves as to the precise nature and extent of the disease, and over the best precautions to take; whether, for example, to call for a gunboat to be stationed off the river to bar all traffic. It was perhaps fortunate that the outbreak carried off no more than 200 inhabitants altogether over the two months that it lasted. Tragically, one of the earliest victims was a man who had enjoyed a brief celebrity as something of a local folk hero, and who was to become one again in the years after his death in neglect and poverty. This was Jack Crawford, who had won local renown by nailing Admiral Duncan's colours to the mast of the *Venerable* at the fierce-fought battle of Camperdown.

Sunderland's generally confused and inadequate response to the cholera outbreak earned it a good deal of contempt. 'More suitable to the barbarism of the interior of Africa than to a town in a civilized country,' the diarist Charles Greville, clerk to the Privy Council, thought the townsfolks' conduct. In fact the danger was not so serious as had been feared, and the outbreak did not spread widely beyond Sunderland. But it did focus national attention on the town and its distressing situation, an example of what Greville called 'a state of human misery, and necessarily of moral degradation'. The controversy and publicity, as Clanny and other doctors involved leapt into print with their observations and deductions, drew national attention to the links between slum

A statue of Jack Crawford (1775–1831) in Mowbray Park

dwelling conditions and disease. It was one of the incidents that alarmed and awakened the conscience of the ruling classes into an awareness of the need to create a new kind of local government, and to enquire into the enormous practical problems that accompanied rapid urban expansion. Yet even after thirty years of progress in local administration, of clearing and re-planning many of the worst slum areas, cholera struck again in 1866 (as it had several times in the intervening years, notably in 1848) and the eighty or so deaths on that occasion were once again confined to the overcrowded lanes that ran from High Street to Coronation Street.

In 1835 Sunderland's local government was at last thoroughly re-organized. For years past the parochial structure had been recognized as inadequate, and in Sunderland as in many other towns it had been supplemented by the appointment of 'Improvement Commissioners'. This body of 150 local worthies had been set up by local Acts of Parliament passed in 1810 and 1826 and given authority to arrange the cleansing, paving and lighting of streets, to organize the watch, and to provide adequate sanitary facilities. One of the first products of the new regime was the Exchange Building, authorised in the 1810 Act and opened in 1814 as a commercial, social and administrative centre for the town, its first 'Town Hall'. Here the Commissioners met, and they did much to make conditions more bearable. It was, for example, in 1824 that they authorized the provision of gas lighting for some of the town's streets, supplied from the gas company's new works in Low Street.

It was the Parliamentary Reform Act of 1832 that stimulated the creation of a new, unified local government. The Act gave Sunderland, recognized as a growing and rich centre of population but hitherto unrepresented, two members of Parliament. The problem arose of defining, or re-defining, Sunderland so as to include its older neighbours; and further of finding a local authority capable of conducting parliamentary elections. There existed the ancient body of freemen and stallingers, claiming their origin from Morton's (and sometimes, with vigorous imagination, from Puiset's) Charter, and exercising authority over rights of pasturage and usage on the Town Moor despite counter claims by both the Bishops and the local fishermen. One of these freemen was prevailed upon by what was known as the 'progressive party' among local gentlemen, headed by the most active of the local business community, Andrew White, to convene a public meeting. There White and his friends organized a demand that Sunderland's rights as a borough be recognized under the new Municipal Corporations Act. Without waiting for statutory confirmation they went ahead with the election of a borough council, and on January 1st, 1836, 'Honest Andrew' White took office as Mayor.

But there was opposition from the county magistrates, who felt their authority threatened by the upstart borough, and from the House of Lords, who threw out the first bill to legalize the new corporation, fearing it as no more than a move to create a new stronghold for a Whiggish local authority. 'Sunderland at present seems to possess scarcely any of the properties of a Municipal Corporation' reported the troubled investigators in 1836. But local pressure and the Whig government in the end carried the day, and on July 17th, 1837, the Act was finally passed which recognized Sunderland's borough status as having existed since the 1832 elections. There thus came into existence a borough government that was to continue until 1974.

The imposing Exchange Building, viewed from the north side of the River Wear

At last the three communities around the mouth of the Wear, long linked by common interests and geography, were united administratively; henceforth they were one, and known unequivocally as the Borough of Sunderland. A fourth community, the flourishing industrialized village of Southwick, might well have been included, as it was for parliamentary elections; but it chose to remain separate until its absorption in 1928.

The new administration was behind the steady development of amenities during the later years of the century. A new police force of one superintendent and fifty-two men was ready for duty by November; it was presumably pure coincidence that they found themselves facing something of a minor crime wave over the next few years, with some sensational murders involving visiting seamen. An adequate mains sewage system was provided during the '50 and '60s, and an increase in the Corporation's powers by Act of Parliament in 1851 paved the way for the clearing of many slum streets and the replanning of much of the east end. Meanwhile the Sunderland Water Company, a Corporation-backed enterprise established in 1846 (it took over the assets and equipment of the Bishopwearmouth Water Company whose activities dated back to 1824), was busily sinking deep wells and pumping up supplies through the limestone, notably at Humbledon Hill in 1846–48 and at Ryhope, 1866–69. By 1869 it could be claimed that 'Sunderland has a larger and better supply of water than perhaps any town in the Kingdom.'

There was already established in the new borough a vigorous intellectual and social life, concentrated in the newly developed area south of the Bridge and especially around the upper end of High Street. Eastern Sunderland might represent the most wretched form of urban life, but elsewhere men lived in a very different atmosphere of spacious leisure combined with wide-ranging interests. As in Birmingham and Newcastle the expanding town and the innovations of the Industrial Revolution produced a group of men, largely self-made, with money and brains and a great urge to self-enlightenment. In Sunderland as in many other towns there flourished active Literary and Philosophical Societies, Debating Societies, Dining Clubs, political clubs, scientific associations, subscription libraries. Doctor Clanny, that vigorous surgeon, scientist and inventor, was a leading figure in this group. His home, where Bridge Street and High Street crossed, was significantly at the new heart of the town. He was one of those who, after the Felling Colliery explosion in 1812, set up the Sunderland Society for the Prevention of Accidents in Coal Mines. His own safety lamp was submitted soon after the disaster both to his Sunderland colleagues and to the Newcastle Literary and Philosophical Society, but it was soon superseded by the more efficient Davy lamp. This itself was the outcome of the Sunderland Society's initiative in approaching the most eminent scientist of the day to request his help, a request that Sir Humphry Davy speedily complied with.

Another prominent and very active figure was Sir Cuthbert Sharp, Collector of Customs in the town from 1823, a distinguished former mayor of Hartlepool. He was the inspiration of a more lighthearted society, the Beefsteak Club, meeting monthly at the *Golden Lion* for 'a feast of reason and beefsteak'. He was well known as historian and antiquarian, a respected member of innumerable busy committees and trusts. Like most of the leading men of the town he was also a very active Freemason; since 1755 when the Phoenix Lodge (whose meeting hall of 1785 still stands) had been founded, the masons had flourished and multiplied, and they played a prominent part in all the public affairs of the town.

Clanny and Sharp were among those who supported the town's Debating Society, Literary Society, and Subscription Library. This last had been founded in 1795 and had some 200 members who paid a guinea a year to borrow from a collection of very learned volumes; and around its rooms in High Street many of the activities of this energetic group were centred. There was little encouragement for frivolity on the part of Library members; 'How degrading it is to the Institution,' wrote the lady librarian, administering a shattering rebuke to a subscriber who had the temerity to request the wrong kind of book, 'if the Subscription Library is to be disgraced with Novels, I will have no share in it.' But for those who sought such lighter fare there was an alternative in the Circulating Library. Perhaps a major factor in encouraging the generally serious and purposeful atmosphere was the presence in the town of one of the foremost thinkers and theologians of his day, Archdeacon William Paley, the author of a number of weighty and widely respected volumes on philosophy, politics and religion, who was Rector of Bishopwearmouth from 1795 to 1805.

The thirst for ideas, knowledge and shared experience was well served by a flourishing body of local printers. It was natural and relatively cheap to print and circulate one's thoughts and discoveries among one's friends and an intellectually

The meeting hall of the Freemasons, built in 1785 in Queen Street

curious local public. Books, pamphlets, leaflets, broadsides, placards, dozens of short-lived periodicals poured from the several presses that had been established in the town since the middle of the eighteenth century; and the little Sunderland of the 1830s supported more booksellers than its much larger successor can today. One leading figure among these printers and booksellers was George Garbutt, who set up in business about 1812 and compiled the first *History of Sunderland*, published in 1819.

An increasing number of schools catered for the educational needs of those in the town who sought some day to share in these literary pleasures. The eighteenth century was the era of the charity schools, and Sunderland was well endowed with such active bodies as the Quakers and the Freemasons. A small but well-known school of this period was that founded in 1778 as the result of a bequest by Mrs Donnison, widow of a prosperous butcher. Moving in 1828 to a building near the parish church, it was intended for the education of girls between seven and sixteen, who were originally taught grammar, spinning and knitting. More substantial schools on the monitorial principles of Lancaster and Bell were being set up from 1808 on; both the established church and the Methodists sponsored such schools. What became the Bishopwearmouth National School was in Low Row from 1808, and Sunderland's Parochial School, next to the old workhouse, was founded in the same year. By the middle of the nineteenth century there were some 140 schools of one kind or another, public and private, taking well over half the town's children. Apart from the packed national and parochial schools most were small, held in private houses or in the churches and chapels. One, founded by the Scotsman Dr James Cowan in 1822 and moved to the Grange in 1830, was nationally famous as one of the major public schools in the North, and might well have continued so; but it disappeared in the years after Dr Cowan's retirement in 1846.

For those in the thriving port who had leisure and sought relaxation there was the theatre. Originally, as far back as 1750, theatrical entertainments had been held in the hall of the Assembly Garth, the centre for every kind of social gathering, balls and dances, just opposite the parish church. From 1778 a regular theatre was established in a disused chapel in one of the narrow streets running from High Street, which was soon renamed 'Drury Lane'. The opening programme demonstrated the varied repertoire of the hard-working actors of the 'Sunderland Circuit', who set out to entertain visiting sailors as well as the local mercantile and professional people; Sheridan and Congreve were mingled with the ephemeral products of such local authors as the favourite actor, James Cawdell, mainstay of the theatre in its early years. In the nineteenth century, when theatres began to multiply, they spread like the other main features of Sunderland's social life to the Bridge Street-Fawcett Street area.

The churches, too, adapted themselves to the needs of a growing population. Within a few years of the dedication of the new parish church in 1719 it was insufficient for the port's needs. A new Anglican chapel was planned in 1764, promoted by the masonic lodges, designed and largely paid for by the landowner, coal merchant and freemason John Thornhill. It was consecrated in 1769 as the Chapel of St John the Evangelist, another attractive brick building, in style very similar to the parish church nearby. With its galleries it held 1,400 worshippers. It represented yet another bite from the mutilated Town Moor, already much encroached upon by enterprising townsmen who dug it for brick clay or to make watering places for their cattle, by quays, wharfs and yards around its seaward margins, and by those who had won permission to fence off plots for building. Close by the new St John's were a number of batteries erected to protect the river mouth and port from the danger of such seaborne raiders as the American Paul Jones; and in 1794, at the time of the French War, a large wooden barracks to house some 1,600 men was built on what had once been the Coney (or Rabbit) Warren in that same northern corner of the Moor; its garrison served to swell the St John's congregation.

The established church might win the approval of the 'Freemen and Stallingers' to occupy common land, but this was not the case for the nonconformists who increasingly attracted Sunderland folk. Since the days of Lilburne and the Parliamentarian seamen a dissenting tradition had survived; throughout the later seventeenth century groups of Presbyterians, non-juring Anglicans, Quakers and, at the other end of the spectrum, a few Roman Catholics, met in private houses. The first dissenting chapel in the port was built in 1711; it may well have stimulated the establishment into sponsoring their own new church a few years later. The building, in Half-Moon Street, near the Corn Market in the High Street, was put up partly in his own garden by George Wilson, who became its first minister. For some time it served for most of those Protestants who had fallen out with the established church, but before the middle of the century half a dozen other denominations had chapels of their own, and the Corn Market Chapel had itself spawned offshoots. There were Presbyterian or Independent chapels at the east end in Robinson's Lane and Maling's Rig, and at the west end in Spring Garden Lane. There was a Quaker Meeting House in High Street. Moreover the Methodists arrived on the scene with John Wesley's first visit to preach before a turbulent crowd in 1743. A 'Society' already existed by the time of his second visit a few months later, meeting in a small room at the top of Swine Alley. It had to change its quarters frequently over the next few years, but Wesley noted in 1752 that it was 'one of the liveliest Societies in the North of England'. He revisited it in all some thirty times before his death in 1791. The first Wesleyan chapel, opened in Numbers Garth in 1759, was moved to Sans Street in 1793; it was speedily followed by several more.

The Catholics, too, emerged into the open once more as the tolerant eighteenth century drew on. True, their first chapel, in a house at the east end of the town in Warren Street, was burnt by a mob in 1746 at the time of the Jacobite threat; but they soon had another, at first in Vine Street and later in Dunning Street, Bishopwearmouth. This was described, however, as 'a dreary loft with a priest's house attached', and since by 1830 the Catholic congregation was growing fast Ignatius Bonomi, the well-known Durham architect, was commissioned to design the new and substantial St Mary's in Bridge Street.

The proliferation of church and chapel went on as new denominations and old sought to follow the spread of population. When in 1851 there was a census of religious establishments it revealed that out of sixty-six Christian places of worship the various Methodist denominations had thirty-four, holding perhaps 40% of the town's faithful. At that time there were ten Anglican, six Baptist, five Independent and five Presbyterian churches, as well as a number of smaller denominations and sects.

One other faith had been well represented in Sunderland since the eighteenth century, when trade across the North Sea had encouraged the settlement of a Jewish merchant community here as in other east coast towns. Vigorous and self-contained, its members were naturally at first somewhat outside the main stream of the town's social and economic development; but by the middle of the nineteenth century they played an important part in commercial and professional life, and had provided themselves with two synagogues.

Provision had to be made for the purely material needs of many among the port's growing thousands, as well their spiritual and social requirements. The fact that the town produced and entertained a large number of seafarers meant inevitably that it was faced with the problem of caring for many widows and orphans; it was for them as well as for retired mariners that the hall and tenements of the Assembly Garth were purchased in 1750. In addition each of the three parishes had its own workhouse, supervised by the overseers appointed by the vestries. They had no easy task; in 1807, for example, the Sunderland workhouse alone held 193 people, while no less than 795 were receiving out-relief and in addition there were 572 'sailor poor'.

St Mary's Church, Bridge Street. It opened on 15 September 1835 and has an imposing 'medieval' façade

One aspect of the consolidation of local government in the 1830s was the creation of a Union of the three parishes (under the 1834 Poor Law Amendment Act) and the appointment of a joint Board of Guardians in 1836. They took over the recently built Bishopwearmouth workhouse at Gill Bridge Avenue and enlarged it for common use. It soon proved inadequate, and in 1853 land at Hylton Road was bought for a new institution which opened in 1855 with 300 inmates. This was primarily intended to deal with the infirm and elderly poor, and it remained well used. The Hylton Road buildings steadily extended their hospital functions and their extent, spreading along Kayll Road until a new main entrance in Chester Road was opened. This former workhouse became the nucleus of the Sunderland General Hospital.

The Guardians of the Poor administered charity tempered by firmness. Parallel with their activities there were a host of private charities and almshouses, of which the most notable was the Trafalgar Square Merchant Seamen's Homes built in 1840. This was intended to supplement the accommodation in the Assembly Garth for the fortunate few among the 800 widows and children and the 300 disabled, worn out, or temporarily unemployed seamen who, on average, lived in the town. The Almshouses were intended for a hundred or so of these distressed families, and they were built in the gardens of the former Sunderland workhouse. Their cost, some £3,000, was largely met out of the moneys raised by the Muster Roll Fund, to which all seamen had long been required by law to contribute 6d. a month from their wages.

Not far from Trafalgar Square an orphanage was built a few years later, open to fifty sons of seafaring men. It was the product of a final charitable fling by the Ancient Corporation of Freemen of the Borough, who were finding their responsibilities steadily whittled away by the destruction of the Town Moor over which they claimed jurisdiction. Docks, staiths and railways encroached in the 1840s, and there was little left to care for or quarrel over. So in 1853, with a last splendid gesture, they allotted the £8,400 compensation paid them by the railway company to setting up the Orphanage on one of the few remaining fragments of the Moor and disappeared in a blaze of charity.

Those who were better off also needed hospital care from time to time, and a variety of institutions appeared in the nineteenth century to provide this. The first infirmary and dispensary was, from 1810, in Sans Street. It was replaced by a roomy and attractive building in Chester Lane,

The decorative plaque over the central doorway of the Trafalgar Square almshouses

built by private subscription in 1822. Paying patients were expected to contribute 10/6 a week, but from 1855 there was also a free accident ward. By mid-century it was proving inadequate and the committee set out to erect a new infirmary in Durham Road; the massive red brick structure of the Royal Infirmary was opened there in 1867. It was added to periodically over the rest of the century, and proudly claimed to be the finest establishment of its kind in the north of England. The old infirmary in Chester Road went on to a varied career; it was for a time a training college for Primitive Methodist ministers and ultimately became a Catholic school.

Other specialist institutions supplemented the Infirmary, an Eye Hospital from 1836, a Children's Hospital from 1867, an Infectious Diseases Hospital from 1892. North of the river a separate Monkwearmouth and Southwick Hospital developed from 1873. Each institution in turn began life in converted or adapted buildings in the crowded streets of the town and moved in time to more spacious purpose-built premises nearer the open country. Each continues its function to the present day.

The new borough that came to life in 1835 was a busy, balanced community. Sunderland had its share of poverty and distress but on the whole its nineteenth-century inhabitants enjoyed prosperity and a wide range of amenities. But the town's well-being rested more and more on a very limited range of industries, and above all on one. It was in the early years of the nineteenth century that Sunderland became one of the greatest shipbuilding centres in the world.

CHAPTER SIX

'A VERY LARGE SHIP-BUILDING, COALY TOWN'

IN the nineteenth century Sunderland achieved world-wide fame as a ship-building town. Three hundred years before it had been one of the many hundreds of fishing villages about the coastline of Britain. Two centuries ago the coal trade and its ancillary industries had wrought a transformation, and a thriving port had grown up. For the past two hundred years progress had been steady though hardly spectacular, as in many another busy provincial seaport. But now Sunderland was entering upon a new phase in its history, one when it occupied a position that was in some respects unique. There was to be a new period of change and growth, and again coal was to be a major factor. But above all it was the development of the ship-building industry that was to give Sunderland the right to claim the position of 'the largest ship-building town in the world'. The claim expressed the pride of those who lived in a flourishing community where ship-building dominated every activity and interest. In 1834 Lloyd's Register of Shipping regarded Sunderland as 'the most important centre in the country', its output almost equalling that of all other ports put together.

As those in so many other small ports, the people of Sunderland had long been builders of boats. Until well into the nineteenth century little elaborate or expensive equipment was needed, and quite large vessels could be built just above the high water mark by anyone with initiative, skill and the money or credit to buy a stock of timber. 'Every place where they can build a ship, almost, is a yard,' said a Royal Commission witness in 1833. Even lack of immediate access to the river bank was no deterrent; in 1799 a small ship of about 63 tons was built on Bishopwearmouth green by a shipwright in his leisure time and in due course dragged about a mile to the water. Very often, as in the case of the Goodchilds and perhaps, earlier, of George Lilburne, shipbuilding was the by-product of some other industrial or commercial enterprise. By the end of the eighteenth century up to fifty ships a year were being built on the Wear, averaging 150 to 200 tons; and in 1798 the famous *Lord Duncan* of 925 tons was launched by Thomas Havelock from his yard at Southwick. The *Lord Duncan*, destined for the Mediterranean and West India trade, was an exception; for most of the Wear shipbuilders the small vessel designed for coastal trade, and especially the collier, was the staple product. Moreover, the typical shipbuilder at this stage was no wealthy capitalist but rather the skilled craftsman combining with his fellows to build on borrowed money and in the hope of a speedy sale.

It was these small groups of self-employed shipwrights who were mainly responsible for the steady growth of the industry in Sunderland, despite occasional setbacks, during the first half of the century. They could claim that their vessels were the cheapest being built, and they drew their customers from London, Liverpool, Scotland and Ireland. They bought their wood on nine months credit, and they could be reasonably certain of a profitable sale before the time came round to settle

A Sunderland shipyard c.1845

with the timber merchant. 'A vessel on the Stocks, nearly ready for launching, about 244 Tons ... a strong, fine-looking Vessel,' read a typical advertisement.

But in the midst of this shifting kaleidoscope of optimistic but short-lived groups that built a ship or two and then dissolved there emerged an element of continuity. All the great family firms that dominated the economic life of the town through its booming days came into being during the early decades of the century; each originated with a man of skill, vision and drive who handed on in time to sons well able to develop their inheritance.

John, David and Philip Laing, Scottish immigrants, set a pattern. They started their ship-building operations on Monkwearmouth shore in 1793 and later, in 1818, moved to Deptford. It was Philip's son, James (later Sir James) Laing, perhaps the most influential of all Sunderland's master ship-builders, who developed the yard into one of the giant firms of the days of steam and steel. But Laing's were in no rush to adopt the new technology when it came; throughout the nineteenth century they built fine East Indiamen and clippers, like the slender and far-famed *La Hogue*, *Paramatta*, and *Torrens*, masterpieces of designer's skill and shipwright's craft.

Another long-lived firm was started by Luke Crown, who was building in Monkwearmouth from 1807. Peter Austin began by operating a repair slipway in Monkwearmouth from 1826, and in 1846 his son Samuel moved the yard across the river to a site just below the bridge. George Bartram built his first ship in 1838, as did

William Pickersgill at Southwick. William Doxford started up the river at Cox Green in 1840, and then opened what became the biggest of the nineteenth-century yards at Pallion in 1857. Robert Thompson was building ships in 1819, but the family did not get started as a continuing firm until 1845, working at North Sands. As J. L. Thompson and Sons the family firm ran another of the great yards of the later decades of the century, while Robert Thompson and Sons, another branch of the family, built at Southwick. George Short was building at Pallion from 1850, while up at Hylton Osbourne, Graham & Co. started work in 1871. All these were names known and respected throughout the world of ships in the proud decades before the First World War.

The early decades of the nineteenth century saw the multiplication of small and generally short-lived ship-building firms; the later decades saw them weeded out until only the few giants remained. By 1840 some sixty-five shipyards were recorded on the river, employing between them about 1,600 shipwrights. In that boom year 251 ships were launched, averaging about 250 tons. The following decades saw a revolution both technological and organizational in shipbuilding; it was a revolution that put an end to the activities of innumerable small firms both in Sunderland and elsewhere. Simultaneously it ended the active life of many a small port whose trade had once rivalled or surpassed that of Sunderland.

It was the speedy development of the railways in the 1840s that sounded the death knell for thousands of the small coastal vessels that had for centuries carried passengers and goods on the most accessible of England's highways. At the same time the emergence of the steamship and of ships built first of iron and later of steel put an end to shipbuilding in any town that lacked easy access to fuel and raw materials, and by any firm unable to reorganize on a much greater scale. Sunderland builders were slow to adapt to technological change; but once the changes were made they were strongly placed to survive and prosper. Inevitably scores of the smaller firms, lacking the enormous capital and the technological adaptability to operate on an enlarged scale, dwindled, amalgamated, or died.

Steam tugboats had been built on the Wear since 1825, and steam packets were a common enough sight, plying regularly from the later '30s along the coast, taking goods and passengers cheaply to London; but the river's first sea-going steamship, the *Experiment*, was built as an ordinary collier of 296 tons in 1845 and only as an afterthought fitted with engines and a screw. Not until some years later, in 1853, were more steamers built, and in 1855 Laing's yard alone launched three. From then on steam steadily displaced sail on the Wear slipways, though the finest sailing vessels, like the famous *Torrens* of 1875, best known of all the Wear's ships, were yet to be launched. But the last desperate bid of these splendid ships to stave off the march of the machine was inevitably doomed, and the Wear's last sailing ship was built in 1893.

Almost simultaneously the transition to building in iron was taking place. The first iron ship, the *Loftus*, was launched in 1852, and the much larger *Amity* in 1853. Few wholly wooden ships were built by the bigger yards after 1863, though many composite vessels with iron ribs and wooden planking were launched, the *Torrens* among them. The last wooden craft was launched in 1880; like the last sailing ship

The River Wear in the late 19th century, looking upstream towards the bridges

it was a Pickersgill product. By that time iron in its turn was about to give place to the larger steel plates.

The development of the steam engine brought a new industry to Wearside as marine engineering firms sprang up. Sometimes, like Doxford's, they were offshoots of the shipbuilders. Sometimes, like George Clark's, the oldest marine engine works still existing, they developed out of a general engineering business. Simultaneously, the development of iron and steel brought a new kind of labour force to the shipyards, and riveters and boilermakers came to work alongside the traditional shipwrights; inevitably there was a certain amount of friction.

The Wear was not in the forefront of the revolutionary changes of the nineteenth century. Most of the first steamers and the first large iron vessels were built where merchantmen and warships had always been built, on the Thames, the Bristol Avon, Southampton Water, the creeks and havens of the south and east and west. But once ship-building became a heavy industry the Wear, like the Tyne, the Clyde and the Mersey, had an obvious advantage. There was no longer a market for small coastal vessels; but the Wear abandoned this former speciality to build the ocean-going ships of its triumphant years.

Production boomed. The result was 'the wonderful picture of thriving industry which the banks of the Wear presented' to the *Daily Telegraph* reporter in 1882, when 'every acre of land is the basis of some great commercial undertaking'. Belching smoke and steam blackened the skies above the river, and coated the town's stonework with grime.

Ships grew ever larger, and as the smaller yards dropped out those surviving employed more and more men with increasingly elaborate equipment. Doxford's in particular launched some of the largest vessels afloat, and from 1893 developed their distinctive 'turret' design for cargo vessels, building a hundred of them in ten years. By the end of the century the thirteen surviving Sunderland yards were launching between sixty and ninety ships a year, adding up to between 200,000 and 300,000 tons and averaging well over 3,000 tons. Ninety-seven vessels totalling 326,701 tons were launched in the peak year of 1906.

The men who built these ships were highly skilled; they had to possess both manual dexterity and considerable strength. They had to face revolutionary changes in the nature of their work and accept an influx of strangers joining them in a booming industry. There were demarcation disputes and ill-feeling, but on the whole the great changes were accomplished without great distress since there was plenty of work for all and generous wages for most in the rapidly expanding yards. It was an age of steam and sweat and noise, of hard work sustained over long hours. Observers wondered at the 'armies of men employed', and 'the prodigious and costly and often marvellous machines and implements used'. The noisy riveting of massive steel plates in particular was a strenuous and demanding task until the arrival of pneumatic tools early in the twentieth century.

Langham Tower. It was built in 1889-91 as an imposing home for William Adamson, a Sunderland businessman whose father was a prominent local shipbuilder

Shipyard workers in mid-century had to keep up a six-day week and a twelve-hour day; this was reduced in 1871, after a five-week strike by the Wearside marine engineers had led the way, to nine hours. They earned wages that were the envy of most of their fellows in less favoured industries, from about 30/- a week in the 1850s (when the usual earnings of an industrial worker were well under a pound) up to 37/- in 1883 and from £2 to £4 in the first decade of the twentieth century, when average wage rates elsewhere ranged from about £1 to 30/-. They were better off even than those in neighbouring shipbuilding centres; in 1882 the Sunderland men were reputed to have wages three or four shillings higher than the men in Newcastle; they were able to gain improvements almost annually, and this in a period when the general level of prices was usually falling.

The numbers at work in the yards grew as men flocked to so well-paid a job. In the 1860s there were some 7,500 men employed in the shipyards and in associated industries like marine engineering, and by the beginning of the twentieth century this figure had climbed beyond 20,000. By that time more than two-fifths of the town's male workers were in occupations relating to shipping or shipbuilding.

But despite the overall picture of growing prosperity there were periods of recession, hardship and unemployment. To protect their interests the Wear shipwrights organized themselves into an Association in 1846; it lasted until 1908, refusing to merge with the National Shipwrights' Association. Strike action was not infrequent, though as early as 1853 a local conciliation board was formed to avert the kind of trouble that both sides recognized could harm their interests, and in general the atmosphere of the industry throughout the nineteenth century was one of co-operation towards increasing prosperity.

The spectacular advance of shipbuilding was the most distinctive feature of Sunderland's nineteenth-century development. At the same time the town's importance as a port was increasing. Its growth was based almost entirely on the shipments of coal, and these in turn were affected by two major factors: the emergence of a network of railways that linked colliery and harbour, and the improvement of facilities in the port itself.

For the two or three centuries of its existence as a coal port, Sunderland had done little more than provide trans-shipment facilities for the keels working down from the busy staiths up at Cox Green, Penshaw, Fatfield, Harraton and Low Lambton. The Wear keelmen were a sturdy, independent breed. Daily they poled or 'puyed' their flat-bottomed boats up to Hylton Ferry, and were hauled from there by their formidable womenfolk on the tow-path. At the staiths they would be laid alongside the wooden staging and covered sheds, and women or girls tipped coals down the spouts from barrows and baskets. Then it was down on the ebb-tide, with a wind behind the square sail if possible, desperately hoping to avoid running aground in the shallow river, and facing the task of hoisting the coal on board the collier vessels. By 1810 there were said to be 750 keelmen and 250 boys on the river, with some 500 coalcasters and trimmers.

The keelmen were in a position to demand substantial dues for their indispensable services and they were ready to strike (as they did, for example, in 1793) if their demands were not met. Coal magnates like the Lambtons and the Vane-Tempests who found these transport charges more than doubling the selling price of their coal sought alternative means of transport and found it ready to hand in the waggonways.

For a century and more waggonways up to ten and twelve miles in length had been in use on Tyneside. In recent years they had become more efficient with the use of iron edge rails, and since 1808 the stationary steam engine had made it possible to haul loaded waggons uphill. In 1815 a waggonway was laid from the Newbottle collieries to new staiths built just above the Wear Bridge. In addition to the normal horse traction and gravity on the final run down to the staiths it made use of stationary engines to haul the waggons over the flank of Hasting Hill and the other heights on its route, while there were new-fangled loco-motive machines operating at the colliery end. Running parallel to the Wear, it was a direct challenge to keelmen, who responded with an outburst of mob violence and arson that was only checked when the local magistrates summoned a troop of cavalry. Thus began a new phase in the history of the port, with Sunderland directly involved in the shipping (as opposed to the trans-shipment) of coal; and the pattern of railways serving the town was to be added to over the next eighty-five years of development.

The Newbottle Waggonway, soon better known as the Lambton (or Earl of Durham's) Railway, was before long supplemented by another from Hetton. Hetton Colliery was a new one, sunk through the thickness of the magnesian limestone in 1822. There were rich seams to be exploited at these hitherto unfathomed depths, but eight miles of hilly country separated the pit from its outlet on the river. To build a waggonway over this difficult country the company called in one of the best-known colliery engineers of the North, George Stephenson; and Stephenson gave them a line that was to remain in use for 137 years. When it was opened in November, 1822, linking the pit to the new Hetton staiths by way off the summit of Warden Law, it employed (along with other means of traction) no less than five of Mr Stephenson's patent travelling engines, which created great excitement. Their success encouraged the proprietors of the projected Stockton and Darlington Railway, who had already engaged Stephenson for their own scheme, to employ this novel means of haulage in addition to the more conventional ones on their epoch-making line. Its opening three years later marked the inauguration of the Railway Age.

By the late 1820s the Lambton and Hetton staiths were playing a major part in the transformation of Sunderland as a coal port. The two colliery lines developed numerous branches, drawing in the output of an ever-increasing number of pits, but they by no means displaced the keelmen, who remained until the 1850s the principal means of supplying the port's coal.

Sunderland by 1830 could claim to be 'in point of maritime importance the fourth port in the United Kingdom', though it was a claim that others would have disputed. But though its two railways added to its trade, other projected lines seemed to be endangering the town's position, and Sunderland faced once more its ever-recurring problem of neglect, its fear of becoming a mere diversion and dead-end, by-passed by the main routes to the north. The Stanhope and Tyne Railway of 1834 carried the coal and lead of western Durham to South Shields, and Lord Londonderry's railway from his pits around Rainton took their coals away from the Wear and down to his new harbour at Seaham, opened in 1831.

'A Very Large Ship-Building, Coaly Town'

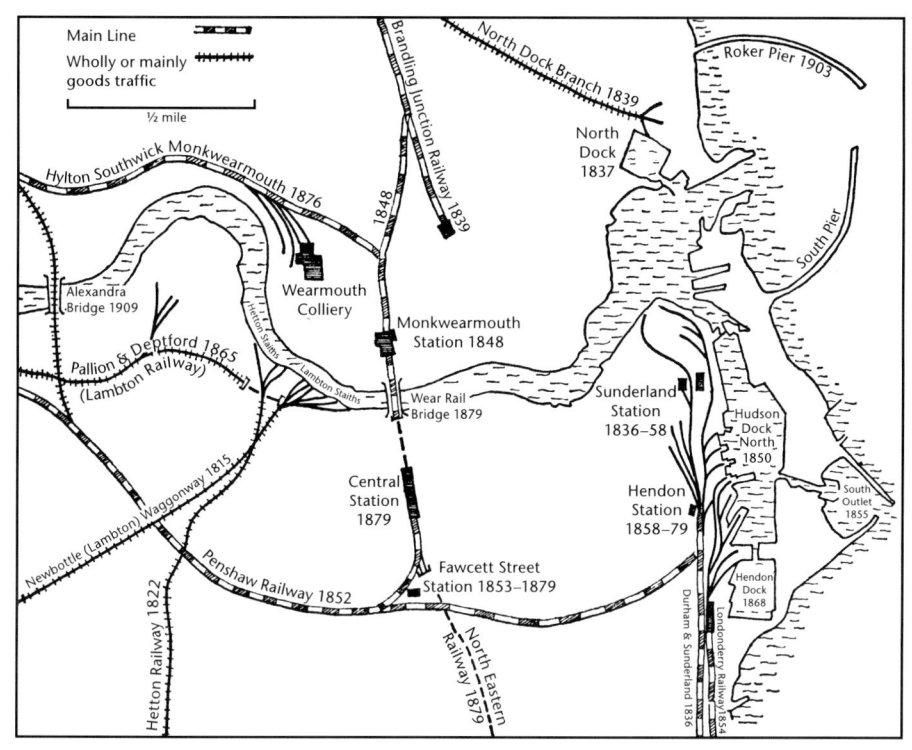

Sunderland's railways and docks

The situation improved in 1836 with the opening of the Durham and Sunderland Railway, worked by fixed engines, which brought the output of many of the big new collieries that were now being opened south of the town to the banks of the Wear. This new coal traffic was hauled through its last stages by a powerful engine on the Town Moor to staiths on the quays; and sidings, sheds and stations virtually obliterated the miserable remnant of that once proud open space. Another railway, the Brandling Junction, from 1839 brought a limited amount of coal to the north side of the river, but its main interest lay in passenger traffic.

With these increased transport facilities and the extension of the Durham coalfield as the deep mines were exploited, the coal exports of Sunderland expanded. Around the turn of the century these had amounted to about 750,000 tons a year. By the late 1820s this figure was nearly doubled, but in the 1830s there was something of a recession, and it was not until 1847 that the exports climbed above the 1,500,000 ton mark.

The new railways could not realize their full potential without fundamental changes in the river itself. The narrow harbour could no longer cope with the traffic, and vessels jostled and queued to enter and leave with the tide. The River Wear Commissioners tried to impose order, penalizing those who failed to keep their stretches of the bank in good condition, and controlling the dumping of ballast, which had long been one of the greatest threats to shipping. Ballast was now deposited well away from the river; at Monkwearmouth, for example, it was taken up a tunnel from the quays to the bank. Other colliers were beached up at Deptford to unload, while still others transferred their ballast to keel boats which shipped it out to sea beyond the bar. The great dumps left in Monkwearmouth, Deptford and Southwick altered the contours of the town, adding sizeable hills of sand and clay. St Peter's Church, once at the crest of a gentle slope, was almost submerged by the massive deposits.

At the same time the Commissioners began dredging the river intensively. An even more significant development was the use of steam tugs from 1825, which speeded up traffic enormously; whereas before a vessel might be held in port by adverse winds and tides for six weeks or more, delay now rarely exceeded a few days.

But clearing the ballast and speeding the turn-round, dredging the river-bed and building piers and lighthouses, did not get over the basic difficulties of lack of room to load and unload; and from the end of the eighteenth century the Commissioners considered plans for building dock accommodation. The matter was made more urgent by the development of new harbour facilities on the Durham coast: Seaham, West Hartlepool and Middlesbrough emerged as new and more convenient outlets for the developing coalfield in the course of the 1830s. Sunderland folk felt themselves being sadly outdistanced in the race to profit from the booming output of coal as Britain moved into a new age of steam and iron.

The issue was complicated by a lack of ready capital, and by the rivalry of those who sought to encourage development on their own bank of the river, north or south. In 1837 the north bank interest, headed by Sir Hedworth Williamson as the principal landowner, opened the North Dock; but it was a puny effort, disappointing its sponsors by its lack of success. The new dock was difficult of access in heavy seas and could accommodate nothing larger than a small collier. The south bank interest, which included all the principal commercial men, coal agents and railway proprietors, remained vociferously convinced that it was the wrong plan.

Their demand for a substantial dock south of the river became the principal issue in local parliamentary elections. When eventually George Hudson, the famous 'Railway King' from York was elected MP for Sunderland in 1845, it was on the understanding that he would press the issue in Parliament and apply his well-known financial wizardry to produce the necessary capital. In return Hudson saw Sunderland as both a base for his political ambitions and an outlet for the extensive railway empire that he was, by dint of various dubious financial transactions, rapidly assembling. Hudson's arrival and his electoral triumph seemed to promise a splendid future for the new hub of his vast interests; there was even a brief intoxicating moment in 1844 when for a few months Sunderland was a link in the major north-to-south railway route that Hudson was devising, and it seemed as though the town might at last escape its chronic fate and never be by-passed by the major flow of traffic again.

Between 1846 and 1850 the new South (or Hudson) Dock was built, excavated from the limestone and protected from the sea by reclamation and embankment. It

Monkwearmouth Railway Station. It was built for George Hudson in 1848

was an enterprise that made Sunderland for a time the most successful port on the north-east coast. Large vessels could, from 1855 on, make their way in through the new southern outlet and avoid the dangerous bar at the river mouth. The Durham and Sunderland Railway erected its new staiths along the dockside and at last showed signs of making a profit for its shareholders. It was soon supplemented by two other lines, the Penshaw link which brought much of the output of the collieries along the Wear, and Lord Londonderry's new line from Seaham to carry the coals his own harbour could no longer cope with. Once again Sunderland's coal exports soared.

But from all this development the sponsors and financiers of the South Dock gained little reward. They got the worst of a long dispute with the River Wear Commissioners as to the latter's right to levy port dues on dock traffic, and in 1859 they were finally forced to make the best of a bad job by selling out to the Commissioners. Hudson, by now despised elsewhere as a fraud and trickster, was still regarded with respect in Sunderland, and the docks he had sponsored continued to serve the town well. For the rest of the nineteenth century they dealt with something more than a third of the town's increasing trade, as coal exports reached towards four million tons a year in the 1880s. Yet local businessmen were concerned that this might have been far greater if the North Eastern Railway had taken over the Docks; as it was, the Railway tended to direct traffic to its own Tyne Dock or West Hartlepool.

Some of the port's coal shipments now originated within Sunderland itself.

The sinking of Wearmouth Colliery had begun in 1826. It was one of the first to follow the epoch-making Hetton Colliery through the limestone in search of the rich Hutton seam, destined to replace the exhausted High Main seam of the older Northumberland pits. R. L. Pemberton of Barnes, landowner and business man, headed the company, and at first the new colliery bore his name. Year after year the shaft was driven down through the limestone and its interbedded strata, meeting constant difficulties with water, which had to be pumped up 1,500 feet and more. Not until October, 1834, was the first worthwhile seam reached, after something between £80,000 and £100,000 had been expended; and in the summer of the following year the first cargo of good coal was shipped out from the colliery's own staiths. Soon 40,000 to 50,000 tons a year were being brought up from what was now claimed to be the deepest pit in the world. At long last, in 1846, the Hutton seam itself was reached at 1,722 feet, and by 1857 the colliery, employing 1,200 men and boys, was producing half a million tons annually. It was followed by other collieries just outside the town, at Ryhope in 1854–60, Silksworth in 1869–73 and Hylton in 1897–1900.

Shipbuilding, seafaring and the coal trade completely dominated the town's economy, to such an extent that by the end of the century half of all the employed men were working in these industries. Few of the town's other trades developed with anything like the same vigour. Many, like the potteries and glass manufacture, expanded in the early years of the century and then went into a decline before its close as improved means of communication enabled specialist manufacturers elsewhere to invade the local market, as overseas outlets disappeared, and as the attractions of shipyard wages and profits drew off local labour and capital. In the first half of the century there were eight or ten potteries along the river, from Maling's in Hylton and Scott's in Southwick down to the 'Garrison' at the river's mouth. Their products, whether plates, basins, jugs, mugs, tea-pots or chamber-pots, ornamental figures for the mantelpiece or decorative motto plaques for the wall, all shared a colourful, cheerful vulgarity and aimed largely at a working-class market, either at home or abroad. It was the decline of the overseas market that was largely instrumental in killing the industry; some 300,000 pieces were being exported yearly in the first half of the century, much of it to Holland; but after 1850 continental tariffs brought decline. The old firms closed down one by one until only three small survivors remained at the end of the century and exports had entirely ceased. The pattern in glass was similar though not so pronounced. The largest firm, Hartley's Wear Glassworks, off Trimdon Street, opened in 1837 and flourished until the '80s, but was closed down and dismantled in 1896. Highly skilled and well-paid bottlemakers disappeared in face of the advance of machine-made glass. However, Sunderland glassmaking, which antedated the potteries, outlasted them and survived in the face of foreign competition; it continues still in two major firms.

Rope-making, another flourishing industry in the early decades of the nineteenth century, naturally lost some of its importance with the decline of sail. About 1793 a Sunderland schoolmaster named Richard Fothergill had invented a machine for dressing hemp and spinning it into ropes and cordage. The machine was actually patented by his executor, John Grimshaw, and after modification came to be widely

'A Very Large Ship-Building, Coaly Town'

The ropery erected at Deptford in the 1790s

used. It supplanted the long rope-walks that figure on the eighteenth-century maps of Sunderland. A 'Patent Ropery' using the new machinery was built at Deptford and still (in 1973) stands there, the oldest industrial building in the town. It was Grimshaw who, in 1824, provided George Stephenson with the ropes needed for the stationary engines on the new Stockton and Darlington Railway.

An obvious consequence of the industrial growth and prosperity was the speedy rise in population. Throughout the nineteenth century it expanded at a faster rate than that of the country as a whole; from under 25,000 in 1801 it doubled to over 51,000 in 1841, doubled again in the next hectic thirty years to over 98,000 in 1871, and rose at almost the same rate to 146,000 in 1901. In the booming 1830s there was an average annual increase of 3%. Workers were flocking into the prosperous town, mostly from the surrounding counties but also from as far afield as Wales, Scotland and Ireland.

To accommodate these hordes of new workers street after street of regimented housing spread north and south of the river. Characteristically the new houses from the 1830s on were single-storey cottages, substantial and spacious enough by the standards of the Victorian working man. They were admired by the government inspectors of the 1840s as 'comfortable and cleanly, and furnished with small yards and other conveniences'. Cottage rows, rank upon serried rank of them, went on being built until the end of the century. Many still stand, at the south end of Hendon, for example, between the gasworks and the railway; and north of Roker

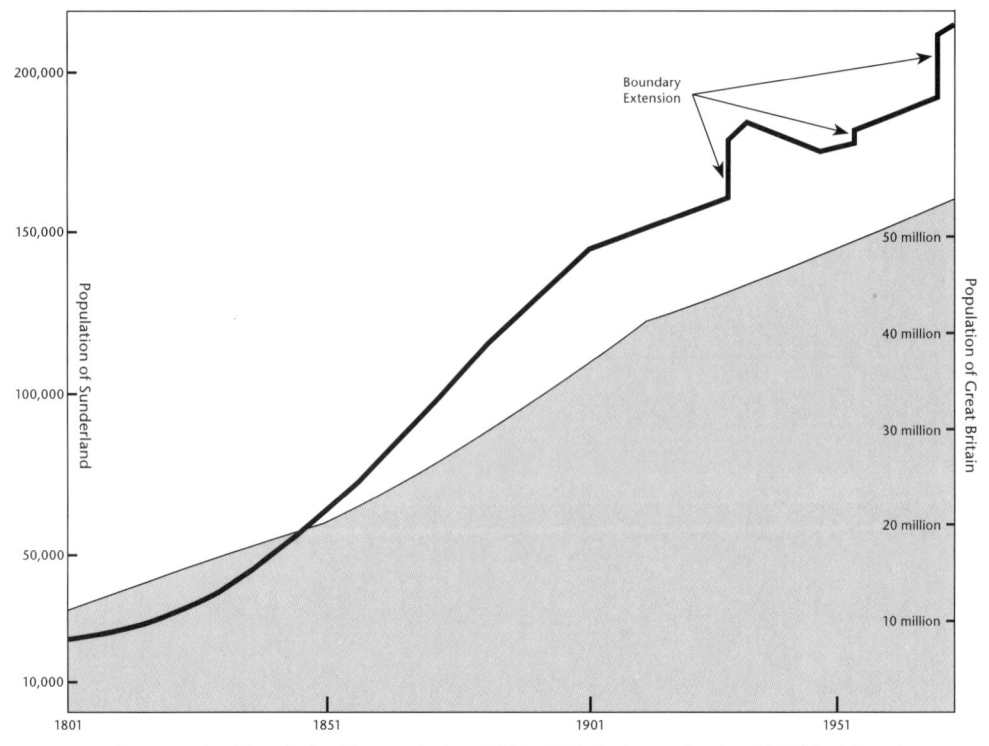

The growth of Sunderland's population, 1801–1971, is shown by the thick black line, in comparison with that of the country as a whole

Avenue, where they flaunt their vintage by bearing still the names of Gladstone's 1880 cabinet: Selborne, Cardwell, Hartington, Ripon, Forster and Bright. From about 1850 similar cottage rows were being built north of Southwick Road for the pitmen at Wearmouth Colliery. Between St Peter's Church and his new North Dock Sir Hedworth Williamson laid out a broad estate in the 1850s with over 400 houses, mostly of two storeys. In the later years of the century less prosperous workers crowded into areas like north Hendon, or those streets north of Bishopwearmouth centre, where earlier housing could be subdivided to accommodate two or three families; and yet others moved into the tight-packed tenements of Sunderland parish or Monkwearmouth Shore, still, despite the clearances and rebuilding of the '60s and '70s, squalid and unhealthy. An enquiry of 1896 found an example of eighty-three people living in the twenty-four rooms of five houses, noted that there were 144 pubs in the east end (one for every twenty-eight families) and fifty-one brothels, and lamented that the women drank harder than the men. By the end of the century the corporation was taking further steps to clear and rebuild this overpopulated area; and in 1903 the first council housing for artisans, the tenement blocks in Silver Street called Harrison Buildings, were opened. They were not attractive, but they were reasonably spacious, soundly built, and supplied with basic amenities.

'A Very Large Ship-Building, Coaly Town'   63

As working-class housing rolled inexorably outwards from the busy centre, the prosperous middle class moved out before it to the town's outskirts, advancing in strength upon the hamlets of Fulwell and Roker or along the roads to Ryhope and Durham. The surge overran and obliterated old landmarks, swamping natural features like Hendon Valley, public pleasure grounds and open spaces like the Valley Gardens (excitingly known, from their popularity with courting couples, as the Valleys of Love) and Victoria Gardens (off Ryhope Road), older scattered farms and rural buildings like the many windmills that had once fringed the town, even the homes of former industry. Everywhere little tangible record of the semirural past was left save for an occasional street name: Valley Road, Old Mill Road, Hendon Burn Avenue, Meadow Vale, Pottery Road, Ropery Walk, Sheepfolds Road, Spelter Works Road. Nevertheless, corporation foresight and private generosity preserved some open spaces even in the heart of the developing town; it was in 1854 that Building Hill was purchased, to become the nucleus of Mowbray Park, and in 1880 that Roker Park was presented to the town by the Williamsons so that Roker Dene escaped the fate of Hendon Valley.

These public parks were lonely survivors in a flourishing town where, inevitably, much that was attractive was destroyed in the name of progress and prosperity. Contemporary visitors could find little of beauty left, and found the scars of industry lying heavy on the town. 'The country is enshrouded in the blackest gloom of smoke before reaching Sunderland' observed *Murray's Handbook for Travellers in Durham*.

As the houses advanced so did the churches and chapels to serve them. Sometimes these illustrated some of the class distinctions of the age: the elegant stone of the little group made up of Christ Church (Anglican, 1866, cost £7,000) St John's (Methodist, 1888, cost £14,500) and St George's (Presbyterian, 1890, cost £12,000), serving the opulent Grange-Ashbrooke area, contrasted with the less ornamental St Mark's, Millfield (1872, cost £4,000) and St Luke's, Pallion (1873, cost £4,100), or the workmanlike brick

An early photograph of the monument in Roker Park

churches and chapels that have now mostly disappeared along with the working-class estates they served. The fact that some of the most opulently decorated and spaciously planned buildings were nonconformist, like the Grange Congregationalist Chapel of 1883 (cost £12,500, including schools) emphasized the emergence into the front ranks of prosperity and confidence of the hitherto cautious congregations they represented. Nonconformity, in Sunderland as elsewhere, was no longer primarily a working-class faith. But Sunderland's most distinguished ecclesiastical building of modern times was a product of the established church; the fine St Andrew's, Roker, was built in 1906–7 by E. S. Prior with the aid of some of the best craftsmen of his day. It served the middle-class residents of what was fast becoming the seaside resort end of the town, despite the fact that according to Murray the area was 'totally devoid of beauty and scarcely out of the smoke of the town'.

The Education Act of 1870 required Sunderland to set up a School Board. When this was duly elected in 1871 it carried out an assessment of the town's existing schools. It found that though there were no less than 11,853 places available already in Sunderland, there were 18,169 children of school age. A prompt start was made in building Board Schools to make up for the deficiency, and James William Street, the first of these, opened in 1874 for 1,050 pupils from the east end of the town. It was speedily followed by others, and by 1880 there was provision for all the children of elementary school age.

For the time being those who wanted a secondary education had to rely on voluntary schools. A new rector of Bishopwearmouth with daughters to educate took the initiative that led to the setting up of Church High Schools in 1884. The Boys' School was short-lived, but the Girls' School, moving to a new building in Mowbray Road in 1888, survived as a permanent feature of the town's educational structure.

The extension of the town demanded development of a public transport system, and it grew simultaneously with the growth of the new working-class estates a mile and more from the jobs on the river and the shops in the High Street. Tramways were laid by the corporation and opened in 1879, leased to and operated by the Sunderland Tramways Company. They speedily extended through all the central area, linking Roker in the north with Christ Church and the docks in the south. By 1895 the corporation was looking with favour on the idea of electrifying the system. In that year the first municipal electricity station was opened, on the site of the old Fever Hospital in Dunning Street. In 1900, when a new and much more extensive plant on the site of the extinct Trimdon ironworks off Farringdon Row was being planned, the corporation took over the running of the tramways and started an electrification programme that was completed within a few years. For another three decades the electric tram remained the principal means of transport within the town, and linked with the Sunderland and District Electric Tramways to provide services running as far afield as New Silksworth, Herrington, Houghton, and Newbottle.

Population and prosperity naturally brought extension and adaptation of the town's public entertainment facilities. Around mid-century the old Drury Lane Theatre became the Wear Music Hall, and a group of new theatres was opened in the

An electric tram at Roker in the early years of the 20th century

fashionable Bridge Street-Fawcett Street area. There was the Theatre Royal of 1853 in Bedford Street and the Lyceum in nearby Lambton Street, opened in 1852. The former enjoyed a long and varied existence, passing from straight theatre to music hall, becoming a cinema in the 1930s and a bingo hall in the 1960s. Through all the building's vicissitudes the stone features of William Shakespeare presided outside. The Lyceum enjoyed a splendid opening, with a charity performance by a group of distinguished amateurs headed by Charles Dickens and Wilkie Collins. It was burnt down, and its reopening in 1856 was afterwards remembered as the occasion of a famous debut; a young man from London who had just adopted the stage name 'Henry Irving' made a not-very-successful first professional appearance in Bulwer Lytton's *Richelieu*. 'A very large ship-building, coaly town', Irving summed up the Sunderland of the 1850s.

    The theatre in Sunderland continued to flourish over the next sixty years. Around the turn of the century the centre of its activities migrated further westwards, and in the Edwardian period a cluster of theatres and music halls enlivened the northern end of the old Bishopwearmouth village. These included the King's Theatre in Crowtree Road, the Avenue in Gill Bridge Road (part of its facade incorporated later into the entrance of Vaux's Brewery), the People's Palace and the Empire facing one another across High Street. The last alone survived long as a theatre, thanks largely to enlightened civic patronage in the 1960s. These were only the major houses of entertainment; small music halls flourished widely on shipwrights' pay-packets.

But a Victorian town with any pretensions needed something more substantial for the gregarious entertainment of the age. The Crystal Palace and the Albert Hall had set the fashion for massive barn-like structures that popular gatherings and concerts, civic fetes and seasonal entertainments, might share with revivalist meetings and political demonstrations. Such a building was duly provided for Sunderland when the ambitious Victoria Hall was opened in 1872. Costing a modest £10,000, it was capable of seating 3,200 and frequently did, though it was never a very profitable investment. Sold and resold, it eventually came into the hands of the corporation in 1903. A £30,000 extension (the Alexandra Hall) was then added, but by that time the days of the great public hall were drawing to a close and it threatened to become something of a white elephant. When a parachute mine destroyed the Hall in 1941 there was no serious attempt to replace it.

The Victoria Hall was the scene of a tragic accident in June, 1883, when 183 children were suffocated and crushed in a stampede, rushing down the stairs to secure a distribution of free toys at the end of what was billed as 'the greatest treat for children ever given'. The disaster aroused nationwide concern and led to legislation over the provision of adequate exits at places of entertainment.

The entertainments of the theatres and the halls were for the evenings, when work was over. In the last decades of the century the idea of an afternoon off, of a weekend, began to spread among workers in Sunderland as elsewhere. Organized sport emerged to fill the gap, and that form of it which most appealed to Sunderland's shipyard workers and colliers was football. The first organization in the town was the Teachers' Association Football Club of 1879, founded by an enterprising Scotsman named James Allan who had just come to teach at Hendon Board School. He was, it seemed, the only man in the town acquainted with the new rules. Two years later the Club became the Sunderland AFC. They played for several years in a ground off Newcastle Road before, in 1898, moving to their new headquarters at Roker Park. From then on the Saturday fortunes of the Club in League and FA Cup matches became a matter of vital concern to most of Sunderland's inhabitants. Early triumphs, when in the 1890s the Club were three times League champions, helped to confirm local enthusiasm and loyalty, and up to 75,000 people flooded into Roker Park on particularly exciting occasions. There are many who would regard the moments in 1937 and 1973 when Sunderland won the FA Cup as the proudest in the town's history.

For many other leisure facilities the corporation took responsibility. It built, in 1877–79, a fine new museum and library to house the town's collections. It provided public parks to replace the receding open air as the town overran the public spaces on its outskirts. Mowbray Park was opened in 1857 and extended a few years later. As the most nearly central of the council-owned open spaces it became both the scene of open-air public gatherings and festivals, as at royal jubilees and coronations and also the setting for an assortment of public statuary. A spirited Jack Crawford was erected about the time of his centenary by a group of public-spirited gentlemen, as was John Candlish, one of Sunderland's more active MPs. There was a tragic memorial to the Victoria Hall disaster and another, from 1922, to the dead of the First World War. But dominating the Park, high on Building Hill, stood

General Sir Henry Havelock, son of a shipbuilder and born at Ford Hall. Renowned in Victorian England for his piety, ruthlessness and devotion to duty in the cause of destroying misguided Indian mutineers, his presence on the hill (where he was long supported by two Russian guns captured at Sebastopol) emphasized Sunderland's pride in the part the town and its sons had played in the building and preservation of the Victorian Empire.

There was a lively awareness in the town of such far-off events. Since 1831 Sunderland folk had been kept in touch with world-wide matters through the medium of a local newspaper. *The Sunderland Herald* and the *Sunderland and Durham Gazette* founded in that year both disappeared within a few years; but they were replaced by a succession of others. Weeklies gave place to dailies. From time to time, especially in the '80s and '90s, two or three newspapers with opposing political viewpoints competed for the town's readers. By the early twentieth century, as national dailies spread their influence and forced the locals to concentrate on purely local news, the *Sunderland Echo* had emerged into the lead, largely thanks to the vigorous proprietorship of Samuel Storey; and from 1914 it was the town's sole paper.

Over all this growth and change the Council created in 1835 presided with increasing confidence, extending its functions and responsibilities as the increasing complexity of the community demanded it. The essential services and amenities needed to transform a crowded urban jungle into a civilized community were provided by these industrious and dedicated Victorians, who laid mile upon mile of sewers, gas-pipes, electrical cables, and tramways; who built schools and

The grand statue of General Havelock (1795–1857) in Mowbray Park

museums and decent houses, who brought some kind of help for the underprivileged and impoverished, and some kind of order and decency for all. They celebrated their achievement at the end of the century by erecting for themselves a new headquarters, designed to be both appropriate to their civic dignity and adequate to house the multiplying functions performed by their official subordinates. They placed their new Town Hall in Fawcett Street, in the heart of the growing town. Planned in 1887, it cost in all some £50,000 and was opened in 1890; its 140-foot clock tower dominated the town and added distinction to what was even then in the course of change from being Sunderland's foremost residential area into its main shopping street. It continued to do so for eighty years, until civic pride and civic bureaucracy outgrew and destroyed it.

Chapter Seven

The Twentieth Century

In the opening decade of the new century Sunderland seemed to have reached a peak of development. Its coal exports soared towards, and in 1904 surpassed, the five-million-ton level. Shipbuilding, too, seemed destined for expansion as new technological developments encouraged the building of larger and larger vessels to meet the demands of growing world trade. The 728 ships launched in the '90s averaged 2,600 tons gross; the 729 launched in the ten years 1900–1909 averaged nearly 3,500 tons. But with the increasing size and complexity of vessels, the uncertainty of investing far in advance of demand led to frequent anxiety about the future of the industry. The shipbuilders themselves, representing the prevailing climate of opinion in the town, voiced their confidence that the long-term trend towards growing world trade favoured their continued expansion, a repetition of the nineteenth-century pattern.

Public confidence found its expression in the new public buildings, dignified and spacious, that ornamented the town centre in the Edwardian decade. They were in style and often in function offspring of the new Town Hall. There was a new Post Office in 1903, palatial new offices for the Wear Commissioners in 1907, new Police and Quarter Sessions Courts, together with a Fire Station, in 1907–1908, and a rash of suburban branch libraries at Monkwearmouth, Hendon and Kayll Road in 1908–9. The new Technical College, opened in 1901, housed the town's most ambitious educational venture; and the new Alexandra Bridge of 1909, linking Southwick and Pallion, was prematurely acclaimed as a triumph. 'In a little while

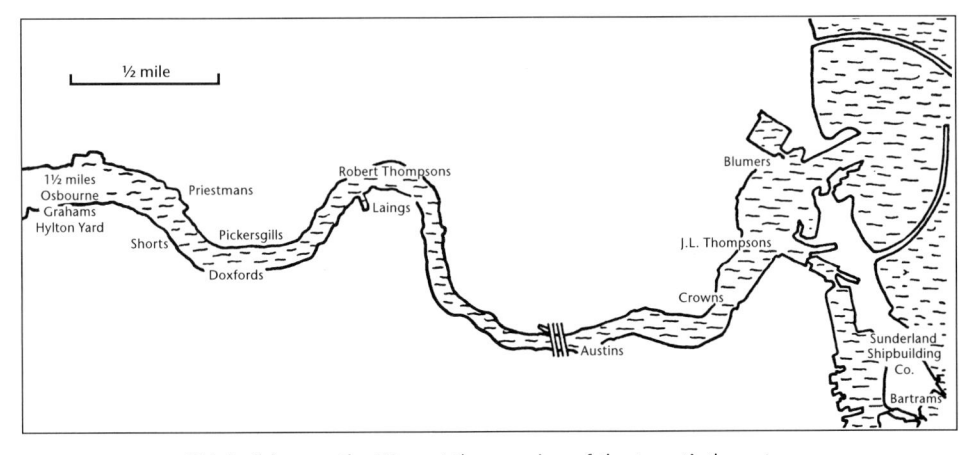

Shipbuilders on the Wear at the opening of the twentieth century

High Street in the early 20th century, looking east

the streets of Sunderland will be known as amongst the most beautiful in the north', wrote a local enthusiast, with some justification.

But despite the town's apparent prosperity there was an underlying fear among those concerned with Sunderland's economic development. It was partly the old-established fear that Sunderland, fractionally off the main north-south route that was now controlled by the North Eastern Railway, and overshadowed as ever by its neighbour, Tyneside, would be the first to feel any recession. As a special correspondent of *The Times* expressed it in 1911, 'The size, population and progress of Sunderland ... have not received the consideration they deserve, and the only explanation is that Sunderland has too many distinguished neighbours on the north-east coast.'

More real and more justified was the fear of overseas competition, of the challenge that had already done much to destroy the local potteries and weaken Sunderland's glass industry. Sunderland folk naturally resented the tariff barriers that grew up in Europe from mid-century on, as well as the new threat from the young and expanding industries of Germany. That continentals should seek to mine their own coal and build their own ships in place of the superior, old-established products that made a living for Wearsiders was perhaps natural, but it was regrettable. Sunderland electors were arguing over the issue of protection for British industry twenty years before this became a national issue of importance; and the danger they had foreseen for so long became all too real in the troubled decades after the First World War.

Another subject that perturbed local prophets was the heavy reliance of the town on a few major industries, and on one in particular. Through much of the

The Twentieth Century

twentieth century those responsible for the economic wellbeing of Sunderland were concerned with the problem of escaping from the industrial strait-jacket in which the triumphs of the nineteenth century had inevitably trapped the town. It was a problem common to many of the cities that had once marched proudly in the van of the Industrial Revolution but now found themselves supplanted by more adaptable competitors, newer technologies, changing demand. The process of adjustment to their new, reduced status was a painful one, and it needed massive state intervention to cushion the harsh effects on industries and workers.

The years 1908 and 1909 gave warning of trouble to come. It was a period of severe recession in shipbuilding and heavy unemployment. Wearside in fact recovered quickly, but the sharp distress, followed by a major strike in the coalfield and minor ones in the shipyards, shattered much of the optimism and complacency that had prevailed in the town. The River Wear Commissioners, the Chamber of Commerce, and the Trade and Commerce Committee of the Council were agreed that fresh industry must be attracted to Sunderland. The three bodies had considerable common membership, all being dominated by the principal local business men and industrialists, and they generally tended to think and act in concert. They identified the problem clearly: 'There is always a necessarily fluctuating quantity of employment in shipbuilding,' and Sunderland's overwhelming dependence on this single employer was, for them, the most foreboding aspect of its economy.

Their efforts had made little headway in 1914 when the coming of War found Sunderland exposed once more, as so often in earlier centuries, to the more immediate threat of military and naval attack. No German fleet bombarded the town, as Hartlepool and Scarborough were bombarded; but until Jutland was fought the danger seemed just beyond the horizon. Instead the Zeppelins came, and in the heaviest raid on the town, on the night of April 1st, 1916, bombs from a single airship heading back to sea after a cruise over the county demolished several houses and struck the tram depot at the Wheatsheaf. One tram was totally destroyed, a conductress lost a leg, and an inspector was killed. In all twenty-two people died and about a hundred were injured.

The direct physical impact of the War on the town was minute. Much more terrible and all-embracing was the death roll of those who, swept up in the Durham Light Infantry, the Merchant Navy, or some other branch of the services, never returned to their families. The dismal casualty lists appeared day after day in the *Echo*, and when on Boxing Day, 1922, the War Memorial erected in Mowbray Park was dedicated it represented nearly one in ten of the 25,000 men who had gone to serve, and the sorrows of almost every family in Sunderland.

Sunderland faced up to the demands of the War in a variety of ways. Temporary hospitals were set up in a number of large houses, the homes of coalowners and shipowners; and at government request a new military hospital was opened in hutted accommodation in the grounds of the Workhouse. Food rationing, allotment digging, money-raising, child welfare: like so many towns Sunderland faced the realities of an emergency. Male volunteers flocked to the colours, women to the hospitals, the factories, even to the shipyards, though in the days when heavy and

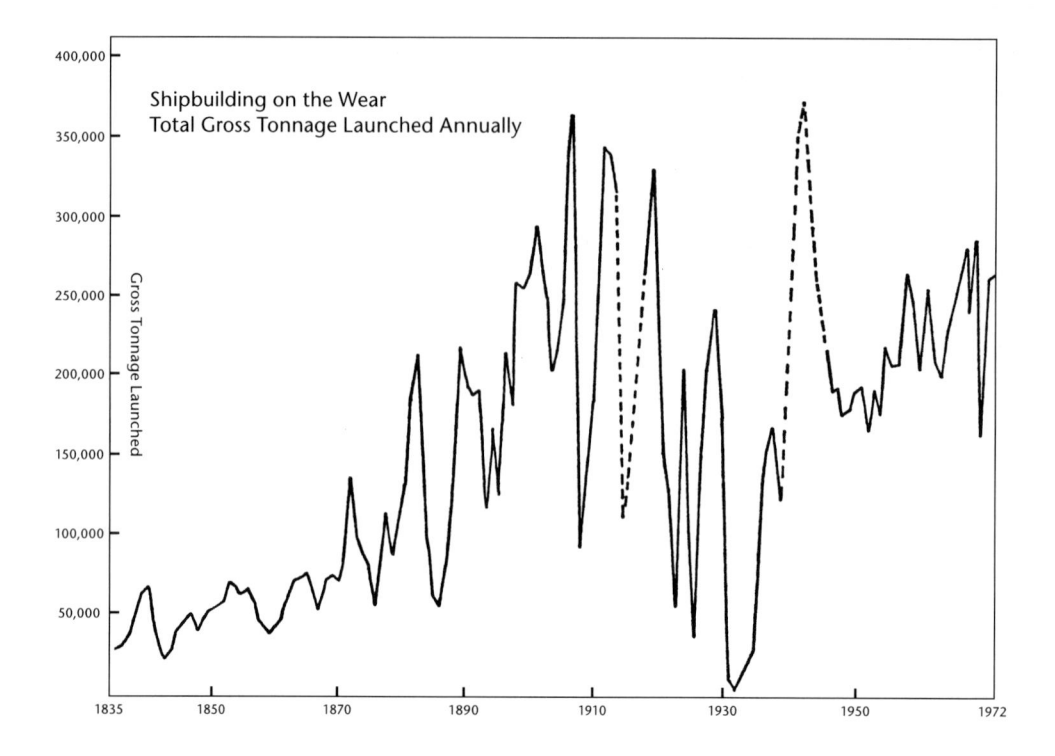

Shipbuilding on the Wear
Total Gross Tonnage Launched Annually

dangerous manual labour was still the major part of a shipwright's job there seemed little scope for them, and in fact fewer than 500 found employment there.

It was of course in the shipyards that Sunderland's principal war effort was made. Naturally the building of merchant shipping dropped sharply in the face of the immediate demands of the Navy, but overall production rapidly expanded until the existing yards were working at full capacity and new ones were opened. By 1918 the need to replace merchant ships was as urgent as the building of naval craft, and in that year sixty ships totalling 267,757 tons were launched. Many were built to standardized designs, though designers and even workers felt some nostalgic regret at this sacrifice of freedom and individuality. At the same time destroyers, troopships, sloops, patrol vessels and lighters were being built for the Navy; Doxford's alone launched twenty-one destroyers and nearly as many more craft of other types. By the end of the War, with steel in dangerously short supply, experimental alternatives were being tried, and one new Sunderland company launched five or six massive barges of reinforced concrete. The inevitable shortage of labour was partly met by importing miners from nearby villages and transferring labour from one yard to another as urgent requirements arose.

With the end of the War many hoped that the shortage of shipping resulting from heavy losses would provide the yards and the town with a prosperous future, and indeed 1920 was a most promising year, when the post-war boom reached its climax. It was indeed one of the most successful years ever, with sixty-seven ships, totalling 333,335 tons, launched. But already there were ominous signs: steel

The Twentieth Century

prices and shipwrights' wages were soaring, forcing costs up to such an extent that shipowners showed an alarming tendency to cancel contracts.

Then came the depression, striking suddenly and with devastating effect. The bottom dropped out of the market for ships as world trade slumped and freight rates fell heavily. By May 1921 four of the smaller yards were closed, and by the summer of 1923 the town had 14,000 unemployed. Three years later, in 1926, there were 19,000 out of work, including more than half the shipyard labour force, and the continued absence of foreign orders was a source of alarm and despondency; in that year only eight ships were launched. Although tonnage on the stocks, launches and employment all recovered to some extent during the later '20s, by 1930 conditions were worse than ever. Then shipbuilding virtually came to a stop; the industry that had created Sunderland and sustained its vast nineteenth-century development seemed moribund. In 1932 only one yard, Austin's, launched ships: two small colliers. Such was the state of world trade that nobody wanted new cargo ships or oil tankers, and these were the only vessels that the Wear was considered capable of building. Government encouragement of the building of passenger ships and orders for naval vessels passed Sunderland by. Increasingly, even when new ships were needed, the world was looking elsewhere than to the North-East, and the region was building less than an eighth of the world's shipping where once it had been responsible for two-fifths. Wearside and English techniques generally were beginning to seem slow and dated, labour too highly paid for the relatively short hours it worked. Wear firms, still privately owned, found difficulty in raising the

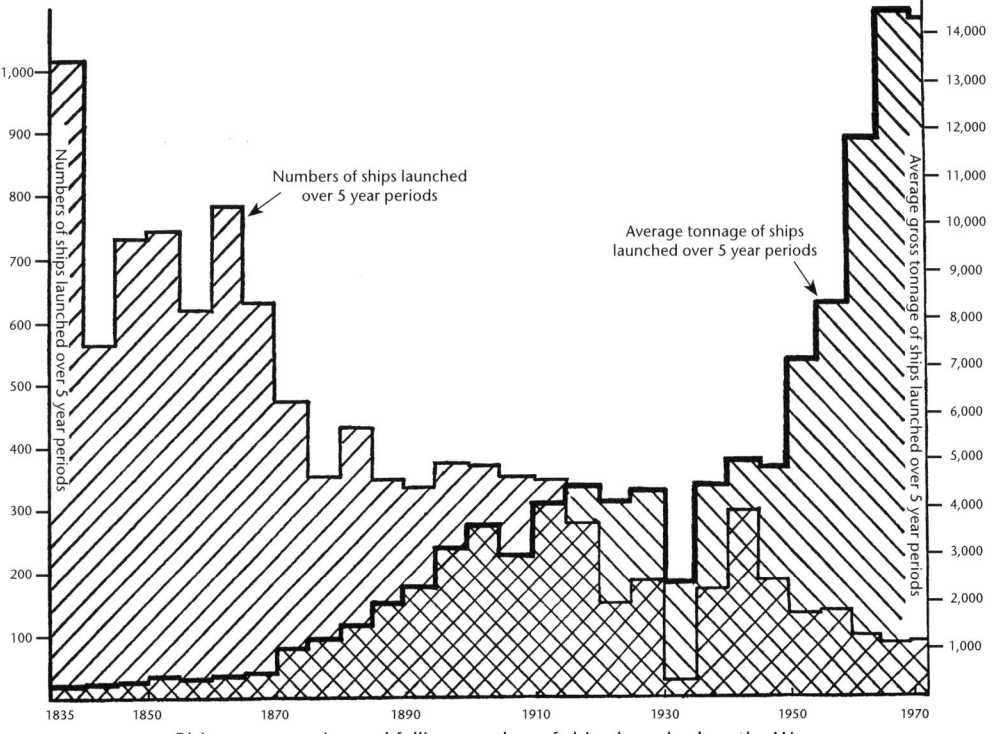

Rising average size and falling number of ships launched on the Wear

capital necessary for large-scale re-equipment and reorganization. The younger shipbuilding industries of the continent and America were formidable competitors for the dwindling world market; and at the same time the locally-based shipowning companies that had always provided the principal market for Sunderland-built vessels were themselves in difficulties as coal and iron exports, their staple cargoes, dwindled.

Unemployment in the yards brought misery. Men spent their hard-won savings, mortgaged their cottages, or slowly and reluctantly left to seek employment elsewhere. Cushioned to a very limited extent by government dole and local public assistance, most preferred to wait in hope of better times, and in 1932 it was estimated that there was still a surplus of 13,000 shipyard workers in the region as a whole, for whom the old jobs would never be available. Nevertheless, for the first time on record Sunderland's population began to fall, dropping from an estimated 188,200 in 1932 to 182,500 in 1939. Where once all had been noise and bustle, the continuous clangour of the riveters and the surge of busy hordes through shipyard gates, now the machines lay idle and grass grew in the berths. British shipbuilders formed a consortium to rationalize their industry, buying up and closing yards to cut down the numbers competing for the reduced market; six Wear yards disappeared for ever in the depression years. Many others kept going only by turning to new trades: shipbreaking, furniture making, caravan and bridge building were all tried as alternatives for the idle yards.

Yet through it all Sunderland shipbuilders optimistically planned for a brighter future, and technical development continued unabated. New ships were designed, and Doxford's developed their famous diesel marine engine, planned as long ago as 1906 and perfected in 1926. It was to play a major part in the transition from coal to oil that took place over the middle decades of the century. Elsewhere, pneumatic riveting and other mechanical aids became general in the shipyards eliminating much of the heaviest and most unpleasant work.

While shipyard unemployment cast a gloom over the town and set the tone of life between the wars, other aspects of the town's development continued with less interruption. The coal industry in the North-East generally was depressed, of course, with output falling from a pre-war fifty-four million tons to around forty-eight million tons in the late '20s and to about forty-two million tons by 1935; but the effects were felt most seriously in the older parts of the coalfield rather than in the new pits of the coastal area. Moreover, most of Sunderland's own coals and most of the shipments from the docks were meant for domestic and gas-producing purposes in London, so the activities of Wearmouth Colliery and of the staiths on the docks and the riverside continued with little check. Although coal exports shrank there was actually a two-million-ton increase in the amount of coal shipped coastwise from the North-East. Wearmouth and Hylton continued to ship nearly a million tons a year, almost all of it for London gasworks; while the major coal company shipping out through the port, the Lambton, Hetton and Joicey Collieries, despatched as much as three million tons from their staiths in some years. In consequence the docks and quays continued, on the whole, to thrive. The port's coal shipments reached a new peak of almost 5½ million tons in the late '20s, and though they fell off miserably in the gloomy '30s, they rarely dropped significantly below the pre-war totals.

A town with something like a third of its labour force out of work, as Sunderland was through much of the inter-war period, had to devise extensive machinery for the relief of poverty. The old Board of Guardians faced an ever-increasing problem, and the town's poor rates shot up as they sought to relieve the widespread distress. In 1930 the Guardians gave place to the local Public Assistance Committee as their functions were taken over by the Borough Council. At the same time the development of government unemployment relief on an increasingly comprehensive, though hardly adequate, scale took much of the responsibility away from local institutions. It remained necessary for voluntary charity within the town to provide help, as it had in pre-war periods of depression. There were voluntary aid committees, boot and shoe funds for poor children, businessmen's schemes to provide children's holidays, food and clothing for the destitute and distressed. The Borough Council took over an old army camp at Seaburn, complete with its huts, for the schools to give deprived children a taste of open-air life; and it inaugurated widespread public works in the hope of absorbing some of the unemployed.

This municipal enterprise during the '20s and '30s did much to transform the appearance and nature of the town. A lot of work took place on the roads, widening, straightening, and replacing setts or gravel with tarmac. The main approach roads to the town were improved, some stretches being turned into dual carriageways. A ring road was completed by 1925; it incorporated the Alexandra Bridge, but neither the bridge nor the road proved really adequate for their task. Another, more successful, new bridge was built in 1928–29, a massive replacement for the elegant old iron bridge of Burdon and Stephenson. It was constructed, its sponsors proudly claimed, with hardly any interruption to the steadily increasing flow of traffic across the river. Public parks were opened, re-planned, beautified; in particular Barnes Park (originally opened in 1909), Backhouse Park (a bequest, opened in 1923), and Thompson Park (1933). The northern suburbs of Roker and Seaburn were encouraged to flaunt their amenities for sea-bathing and sun-bathing, and the council supplemented these with promenades, cliff-top gardens and walks, a fairground and a large public hall opened in 1939 for dances and concerts. The former Workhouse, taken over from the Poor Law Guardians to become the Municipal Hospital in 1929, added to its functions and its buildings, developing specialist medical units as well as keeping responsibility for the elderly and destitute who had so long been its inmates. The town's street lighting was changed from gas to electricity during the '20s. The tramways, after some heart-searching over the desirability of scrapping them altogether in favour of motor buses, were reorganized under a new manager from 1929, speeded up and modernized. They lasted for just another 25 years; the buses had been introduced to supplement their service in 1928 and finally began to displace the trams in 1950, when lifting and scrapping of the lines began. In 1954 the last tram in the North-East made its ceremonial farewell run from the Town Hall to Seaburn and back to the Wheatsheaf Depot.

The council was active in a more direct effort to improve the economic advantages of Sunderland. On the river it shared responsibility with the River Wear

Redby School children photographed in July 1935

Commissioners; the two bodies worked in harmony, and from 1938 corporation representatives dominated the membership of the Board of Commissioners. The RWC had, in the last years before the War, almost completed work on the two outer piers to protect the harbour, with a new lighthouse to mark the entry to the river. Between the wars it was the council that initiated and, with government aid, financed the major improvement in the river's facilities. Between 1927 and 1934 a long new deepwater quay for general cargo replaced the old Low Quay and Commissioners' Quay, transforming the southern bank of the river. The building of Corporation Quay destroyed many small wharves and a cluster of crowded old houses, taverns and workshops that had given the riverside much of its colour, character, and atmosphere. It was part of the new century's purposeful quest for organization, efficiency and large-scale operation. Over a thousand feet long, the new quay was provided with concrete warehouses and a row of electric cranes. Higher up the river a new Fish Quay was subsequently added; but despite the facilities provided for it the remains of Sunderland's fishing industry were fast disappearing, and within a few years the Fish Quay ceased to be used for any specialist purposes.

It was in the field of housing policy that the town council displayed its most welcome initiative, after a very hesitant start. The Sunderland of the inter-war years retained its reputation for overcrowded and inadequate living conditions. In 1926 it was reported that Monkwearmouth alone still had 123 one-room tenements, with an average of over four people living in each, and seven, eight or even eleven in some rooms; in the same area ninety-three cellar-dwellings were occupied, and many of these and other homes suffered from frequent flooding caused by old wells and sewer overflows. The Registrar General's report on the 1931 census described Sunderland as one of the most overcrowded towns in the whole country, with some 30% of its people living in undesirable conditions; another check in 1936 found 20.6% of Sunderland's families to be overcrowded as compared with a national average of 3.8%; and in neither case was the definition of 'overcrowding' a particularly rigorous one. With these conditions, ill-health and high death-rates persisted; nearly twice as many people died in Sunderland from tuberculosis compared with the national average, and an infant mortality rate of ninety-two per 1,000 (in 1935) compared unfavourably with the national figure of fifty-seven. To be born in the slums of Sunderland was a guarantee of poor prospects for future health and welfare.

The Council slowly bestirred itself to remedy the situation. The slums of the Sunderland parish area were slowly cleared, and its crowded population dropped fractionally by 1931, more substantially in the '30s. Government pressures as a result of the damning statistics and attendant publicity led to a speeding of the clearance programme, and nearly half the people of the east end were moved from what had been the hub of trade and prosperity to new estates on the fringes of the town. In some of the cleared areas the North Eastern Housing Association, in co-operation with the Council, built rectangular blocks of flats, the rather gloomy brown brick masses of the 'garths'.

Beyond the built-up outskirts of the town the Council began in a modest way to initiate its own housing programme. It had bought land for this purpose, 162 acres of it in the Plains Farm area, during the last year of the War; and here, at first in co-operation with the Housing Association and later independently the Council began its building programme. Not until 1926 were the first corporation houses ready for letting; in Stamford Avenue on the small Humbledon Estate. They were speedily followed by others at Leechmere, in Monkwearmouth, and, from 1929 on, in the extensive estate developed in and around the grounds of the demolished Ford Hall. Later another estate grew across the river at Marley Potts, and by 1939 the corporation could claim that it had erected 4,682 houses, 102 flats and 173 bungalows, while another 1,594 houses and 540 flats had been built for it by the Housing Association. In all the corporation controlled some six thousand properties, for the most part in self-contained estates with their own shopping centres and provision for social services.

In another respect the corporation extended its responsibilities, and 1928 saw a considerable extension of the boundaries, notably to take in Southwick village. The outward surge of housing, privately built as well as council sponsored, continued in every direction to fill up the new acquisitions and press beyond; an almost complete circuit of new estates appeared in the '30s, and while the new council housing was generally to the west, along the lines of the Hylton, Chester and Durham roads, it was supplemented by the development to north and south, nearer the coast, of rather more substantial semi-detached housing for private occupation. In the south this extended along and beyond Queen Alexandra Road; in the north it was

A street on the Marley Potts housing estate

more extensive, pushing out through Roker and Fulwell on towards the village of Whitburn, where the Seaburn estate was developed in the period just before and after the Second World War.

Perhaps surprisingly, the inter-war depression seems to have bred little industrial and political discontent in Sunderland; helpless apathy was a more common reaction. The shipyard workers in particular, with memories of their past as an industrial elite and loyalties to family firms, were less left-wing than might have been expected. The Labour Party in the town had been strong enough to capture one parliamentary seat as far back as 1906, but was ousted in the election of 1918; and although there were two Labour MPs in 1929, both went down with their party two years later. For all but those two years Sunderland was represented between the wars by Conservatives or their allies. Labour representatives gained more success in their challenge to the public-spirited and traditionally non-political industrialists and business men who continued to dominate the Council; they introduced a party political element previously absent from local elections and forced their opponents to declare their loyalties. For three years from 1935 Labour representatives controlled the borough, and they returned triumphantly for a more extended period of office in 1945, facing the challenge of the post-war years.

The General Strike of 1926 saw in Sunderland none of the rioting, violence and sabotage that took place elsewhere in the North-East, at Newcastle, Gateshead and

Killingworth. The machinery set up by the government to meet the emergency at local level moved smoothly and speedily into operation. The Organization for the Maintenance of Supplies, the Voluntary Service Committee, the Government Transport Committee, the Emergency Officer for the Distribution of Coal all began their activities on May 1st, as the Strike became unavoidable, and in a very short time posters calling for volunteers were all over the town. Over 3,000 men signed on at the recruiting centre in the Victoria Hall during the first week of the Strike, offering help to maintain food supplies, transport and communications and to carry on essential work.

In contrast the trade unions seemed ill-organized. The miners at Wearmouth, Hylton and Silksworth were out solidly; and the only violence in the district occurred at the last of these when, in October and long after general support for the miners had collapsed, three or four blacklegs attempted to return to work, causing much ill-feeling, stone-throwing and police baton charges. Other workers were not so certain of their cause, and conflicting orders from the TUC did not help matters. The municipal transport system closed down completely, though a few private buses continued to run. Electricity and gas supplies, however, were kept going by the technical and managerial staff. The *Echo*, though reduced, was able to publish daily. It now took a firmly Conservative line, having abandoned the radicalism of its earlier days as its recently deceased proprietor, Samuel Storey, had grown old and mellow. It dutifully published daily the official and somewhat misleading bulletins put out over the government controlled BBC. A few trains, manned by volunteers, kept open communications with Newcastle and the south; before the Strike was over trains were running fairly reliably every hour. Such shipyard workers as had jobs continued at them. The breweries, after much debate and shilly-shallying, were finally forced to close down, though mysteriously there was no consequent shortage of beer. The postal service was cut to a mere two deliveries daily. But boot and shoe repairers were able to report boom conditions, milk supplies were kept up, and, though some prices soared, food supplies were generally satisfactory. A few people seemed ready for trouble; two men were fined £20 each for forcefully obstructing a van giving lifts near Fulwell Mill, and a miner who assaulted a road-worker was fined £1 though he pleaded drunkenness. But in general by May 11th, when the Strike drew to a close, men were drifting back in most industries, and Sunderland could congratulate itself on its tranquil record.

Towards the end of the inter-war period there came positive government action to encourage the development of new industries in the worst-hit areas. North Eastern Trading Estates Ltd was set up and financed by the Board of Trade in 1936 to buy land, lay on services, build factories and rent these as ready-made premises to any industrial firms that could be persuaded to move into the area and provide employment. Their initial and most spectacular achievement was the Team Valley Estate, where they set up their headquarters. In Sunderland the Company began development of the Pallion Industrial Estate in 1938, and four firms were established there before War broke out. The Estate expanded after the War, and a variety of light industries did something to reduce the excessive dependence on shipbuilding for employment. Similar developments supplemented it later at Southwick, Hendon and Pennywell. A host of new factories appeared; they produced among other things aero engine parts, scientific equipment, furniture, electronic gadgetry, clothing, telephones; indeed, almost anything that the consumer society of post-war Britain could want. The scheme was superficially highly successful, producing neatly planned estates of clean, busy factories; but its critics pointed out that this new kind of industry tended to employ women rather than displaced men, and that since the new factories were usually branches or subsidiaries rather than parent firms they were more easily sacrificed and liable to be closed down in periods of recession. Still, the rectangular boxes of concrete, brick and glass extended to Sunderland the uniform veneer of twentieth-century consumer industry, replacing much of the outmoded smoke, dirt and clangour that had characterized the town's more earthy and individual past.

The depression period saw the spectacular rise of the cinema as a cheap entertainment for the long hours of enforced leisure. It had first appeared in Sunderland in 1906 when an enterprising (and subsequently famous) showman named George Black converted the former Bonner's Field Presbyterian Chapel, at the north end of the Wear Bridge, into what he claimed was 'the first permanent cinema north of Birmingham'. Its first audience, in wooden chapel pews, saw *The Launching of the Mauretania*. Known at first as the Monkwearmouth Picture Hall, it was eventually re-named the Bromarsh Cinema, and continued until bombed in 1941. Within a year or two of its opening there were picture halls or electric palaces all over the town: at the Wheatsheaf, in Villiers Street, at the former Star Music Hall in Sans Street and at the former Olympia Skating Rink in Holmside. Music Halls like the Palace and straight theatres like the Avenue, finding their audiences seduced, were forced to rely on variety interspersed with films. 'A few years ago we had musical comedy, drama, operas, Shakespearian plays, etc ... Now we get varieties and pictures,' lamented a Wearsider in 1912, regretting 'the all conquering moving picture' where 'comfortable seats can be had for twopence or threepence'. By the mid '20s only the Empire ran straight plays or musical comedies; the Avenue, the Kings, and the Palace all mixed films with variety turns, and eight or ten cinemas scattered throughout the town centre and outskirts served undiluted melodrama and knockabout, Valentino, Pickford and Chaplin as an escape from the realities of depression. In the '30s two palatial super cinemas were built; but soon after the Second World War the day of the cinema ended, and in the '50s Sunderland cinemas began to close until, in the mid '60s the town was reduced to four struggling survivors.

By 1939, with unemployment down to a mere 21%, the long depression seemed, at least to optimistic observers, to be giving place at last to some sort of recovery. Then came the Second World War, and Sunderland was exposed once more to bombardment from the air; despite it, the shipyards again played a major part in the war effort.

This time the bombing was much heavier and more prolonged. Starting in 1940, it went on with monotonous regularity through most of 1941. The casualties mounted, and among the buildings destroyed was the Victoria Hall. 1942 was comparatively quiet, but in 1943 the raids reached a peak of intensity with two

The Twentieth Century

savage attacks on May 16th and 24th that destroyed much of the central area. In fact Sunderland was the most heavily bombed town in the North-East, and the districts that suffered worst were the crowded streets west of Fawcett Street rather than the docks and shipyards; though J. L. Thompson's yard was in fact severely damaged in the final devastating raids and production was held up for some time. In all 267 people died in the course of 35 raids, and 362 were seriously injured. In addition to the Victoria Hall a number of major buildings suffered severely: the central station, St Thomas's and other churches, several cinemas and major stores. The town bore the scars in its flattened heart for more than two decades. Over a thousand houses were completely destroyed, nearly 3,000 more were so badly damaged as to be virtually useless, and 32,000 suffered slight damage.

Meanwhile the shipyards responded to the demands of wartime. Again their contribution was mainly in the building of merchant shipping, and Sunderland

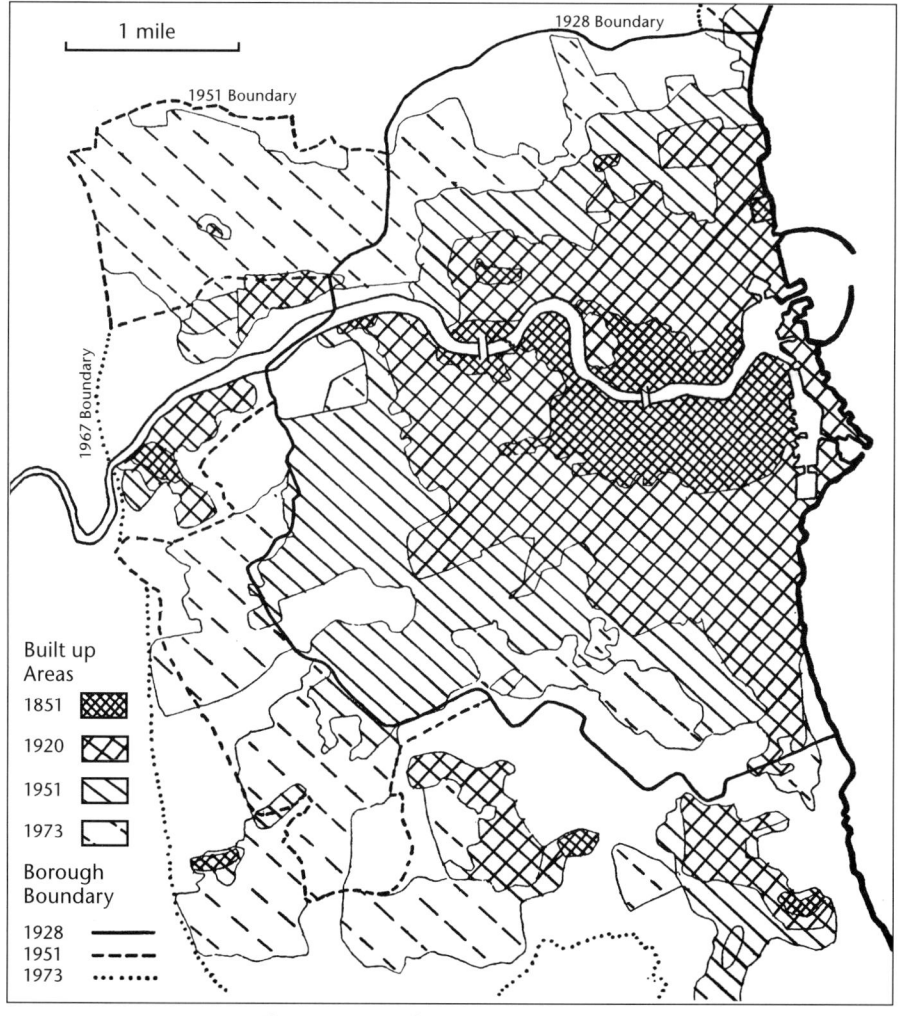

The expansion of Sunderland, 1851–1973

could claim to have supplied 27% of the United Kingdom's total production of merchant vessels. In 1942 fifty-eight ships, totalling 374,794 tons were launched, the highest tonnage ever on the river. In all more than a million and a half tons were launched during the War as the Wear yards speedily adapted themselves to the need for mass-produced, standardized merchantmen to replace the convoy losses, and Doxford's alone were able to launch seventy-five ships, amounting to over half a million tons. New techniques were adopted, notably the widespread use of welding and the prefabrication of large sections, which involved the re-training of labour and re-organization of the yards and buildings; though these new methods had by no means completely displaced the more traditional techniques of riveting before the end of the War. Welding was a skill that could be learnt by women workers, who played a much more significant part in the expanding labour force than they had in the First World War. Meanwhile, naval work in the river concentrated on the building, fitting out and repair of convoy escort vessels, corvettes and frigates, with landing craft of various kinds. There was co-operation, too, with overseas shipyards: a standard design of cargo ship evolved on the Wear by J. L. Thompson and Sons was adopted, after a visit by the firm's managing director to the USA, as a prototype for the 2,700 'Liberty Ships' subsequently mass-produced by American and British yards during 1942–45.

The war years were, for everybody, a time of intense effort, full employment, and strain, coupled with a nagging fear that, when peace came, those long-term tendencies that had already made themselves evident would he re-established in Sunderland's basic industries. In fact post-war conditions ensured that it was not until the '60s that the pattern of slump conditions was restored; for the time being world shortages meant continued demand for Sunderland's products. This was particularly evident in the shipyards, where the major worry for the first ten years of peace was not so much shortage of orders as shortage of steel supplies; and for a time this lack severely restricted production. No sooner did this situation ease than the dreaded foreign challenge reappeared in the formidable shape of Japan, whose yards were ready and able to adapt themselves to the new demands for great oil tankers and bulk cargo carriers. In the nineteenth century Britain had virtually monopolised world shipping production; between the wars she had still dominated a dwindling market; now, in 1956, she finally lost her place in the forefront of world construction as Japan, soon followed by Germany, took the lead. By the middle 1960s Britain was producing barely an eighth of the tonnage of her principal rival: it was a complete reversal of the position in the previous century, when Britain had as far outstripped all her competitors. Japanese yards, with plenty of capital, a flexible working force, powerful and imaginative management, and technological ingenuity, were well adapted to meet the enormous new demand created by the radical change in the pattern of world trade, the demand for ever larger and simpler super-carriers.

It was not that the Wear yards lacked initiative or adaptability; rather they lacked capital and space. In the immediate post-war years the wartime extension of welding and prefabrication techniques was carried on to its logical conclusion; this involved new buildings together with sophisticated machinery for cutting and handling plates and prefabricated sections. New yard layouts had to be devised, and this gave fresh stimulus to the continuing processes of amalgamation and rationalization. Austin's and Pickersgill's combined in 1954, Laing's and J. L. Thompson's were linked in the Sunderland Shipbuilding, Drydocks and Engineering Company in the same year; and this in turn amalgamated with Doxford's in 1961 to form the massive Doxford and Sunderland Shipbuilding and Engineering Company; then, in 1972, the whole group was taken over by an outside organization, the Court Line, becoming known as Sunderland Shipbuilders, Ltd. The Court management promised an infusion of new ideas, a much needed reorganization and rebuilding of the yards. Other Sunderland firms, Crown's, Short Brothers, and Bartram's, either disappeared or were taken over in these years of rapid change. Year by year the number of berths on the river declined; but each year those remaining produced ever larger vessels.

It was at the North Sands Yard, belonging to J. L. Thompson & Sons, and subsequently to the Doxford and Sunderland group, that the most spectacular of the new vessels were constructed. Facing down the lower reaches of the river towards the open sea, it had the berth best placed for launching the massive, squat bulk carriers that the '60s demanded; even so, the ships appeared far too large for the river, and could only be launched with care, skill, and elaborate precautions to avoid damage to themselves or to the banks. In 1963 the *Borgsten* set a new size record for the river of over 50,000 gross tons (its tonnage, as with all the new cargo vessels, was more usually quoted as deadweight—86,800 tons; but this was slightly misleading in

The *G.M. Livanos*, launched by J. L. Thompson on 26 April 1968. At 47,000 gross tons, it was one of the largest ships built on the Wear

comparison with earlier tonnage figures); in 1971 the *Orenda Bridge* reached 70,400 gross tons, and in 1972 the *Naess Crusader*, 84,500, or 158,000 tons deadweight.

The other major group on the river, Austin & Pickersgill, devised another successful answer to the challenge of world competition. They concentrated on the development of a new standard design for a tramp cargo carrier of around 9,000 tons, intended to replace the worn-out 'Liberty Ships'. Production of this shelter-deck vessel, the SD 14, began in 1966; by 1971 they were being launched at a rate of one every 52 days from the Southwick yard.

A very similar pattern of change took place in the post-war activities of the port. At first the fall in the exports of coal was a slow one, and in the early '50s Sunderland was still shipping over three million tons annually of her staple export. In the later '50s a massive reconstruction of Wearmouth Colliery was begun with the object of

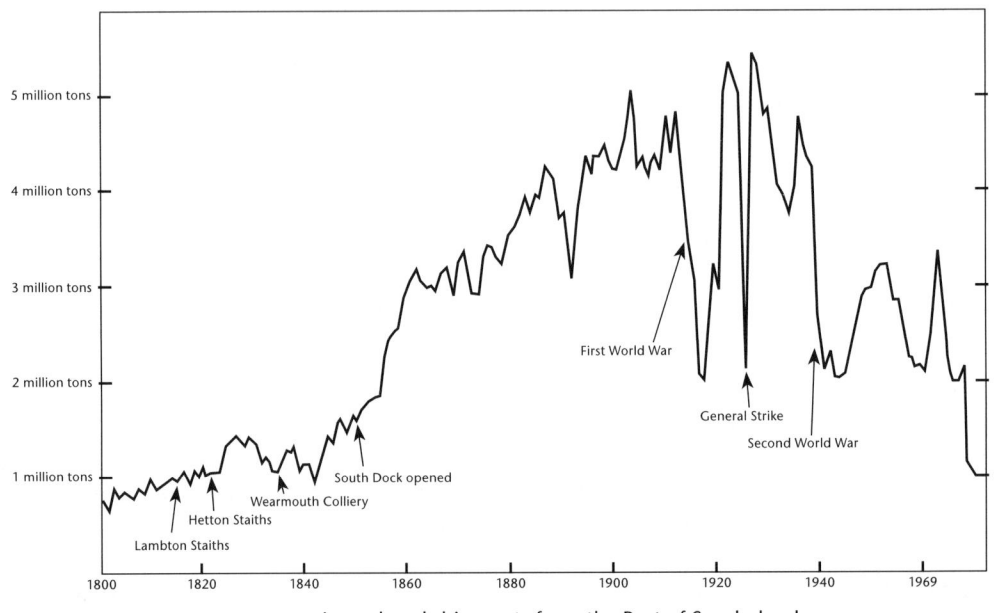

Annual coal shipments from the Port of Sunderland

exploiting more fully the under-sea seams and reaching an eventual output of a million tons a year. But by that time the coal industry too had been hit by economic change, and many collieries were being closed as part of the NCB's rationalization programme or had ceased to ship out by way of the Wear. In 1959 the old railway from Hetton Colliery closed down, and in the course of the 1960s the Lambton and Hetton staiths, which had inaugurated Sunderland's coal shipments 150 years before, finally passed out of use. Coal shipments fell to little more than two million tons by 1960. The nearby pits of Ryhope and Silksworth closed in 1966 and 1971 respectively; and as the demand for gas coal fell away in the face of natural gas so coal shipments dwindled to barely a million tons by 1971. Increasing imports partly offset the effects of the decline in exports, bringing new adaptation in the port facilities; these were mostly of raw materials for use in local industry, and in particular the docks developed as a terminus, storage and distribution point for oil shipments.

Inevitably the changing pattern brought reduced employment; fewer men were working in the shipyards, mines and docks. The once crowded yards needed only some 9,000 men in all by the mid '60s. The decline was slow enough, and the build-up of alternative industry strong enough, to avert the massive redundancies of the '30s. The general policy of government was now firmly set on the lines evolved between the wars: the economy was to be moulded to suit the worker, and industry and employment was to be provided in the Development (formerly depressed) Areas at the expense of the consumer and the taxpayer. Even so, unemployment in the town, as in the North-East generally, remained consistently above the national average. In the '40s it was down to a mere 4%, but by the later '60s it rose towards the 6% to 8% range, and in 1972, with over 10,000 unemployed, Sunderland's rate of 11.4% was double the national one. It seemed as though the disastrous depression of the '30s might be repeated; worried shipbuilders, facing an uncertain future, appealed to the government for the kind of massive aid that had been granted already to other centres of the industry like Belfast and the Clyde.

But if the economic basis of life in Sunderland in the third quarter of the twentieth century was somewhat shaky there could be little doubt that in many respects the quality of life in the town was changing for the better. Something of the old isolation of the town disappeared; in a purely physical sense this was achieved with the major improvement of the road links, long inadequate in the eastern part of County Durham, brought about as a result of government policy of the 1960s. Fast dual carriageways linked Sunderland with the Durham Motorway by 1969 and with Teesside by 1971. On the other hand plans to develop the former RAF fighter station at Usworth into a municipal airport after its purchase by the Council in 1962 matured slowly, and the railways played an ever-dwindling part as the link with Durham closed, docks traffic fell, and direct trains to London and the south came to an end.

The most obvious and impressive success of the Borough Council in the post-war decades was in its housing programme. This was coupled with the final enthusiastic (some argued it was over-enthusiastic) demolition of the older slum areas, which left vast stretches of the east end as desolate, empty ground. The town faced a need in 1945 for a total of about 12,800 homes to replace houses destroyed or damaged by German bombs, to clear the remaining slums, and to re-settle at a lower density those still overcrowded in the east end and in Monkwearmouth. The Council made immediate plans to put up nearly 1,000 temporary houses and some 3,000 permanent ones in the next two years, and by 1947 a vast programme was under way. A start was made at the Springwell Farm Estate, and Thorney Close soon followed. Sunderland could take pride in the building activity that followed, placing her at the head of the league table of towns with post-war council housing. More than 20,000 houses in spreading estates were built in the twenty years after the War, acre upon acre of red brick stretching over the green fields and farms that had once surrounded the town.

Sunderland almost doubled its built-up area, and the change was recognized in the extension of the borough boundaries that took place in 1951 and again in 1967; in this last and greatest growth the town took within its bounds the former villages of Ryhope, Silksworth, Herrington and South Hylton. A fresh expansion of building, a complete new suburban town at Doxford Park was envisaged and begun, but some of the emphasis in this later phase of council building was switched away from the semi-detached house to the construction of multi-storey flats in the east end, Monkwearmouth, and the 1964–67 estate of Gilley Law.

If the town, thus renewed, was much more extensive, it was also much cleaner. Smoke control imposed on the central area in 1960 was soon widely extended. Public buildings were scrubbed and cleaned, half a century of uniform black grime giving place to pallid, unfamiliar grey or mellow brown. A new town centre shopping precinct took shape, after much delay, between 1966 and 1969, together with three tall blocks of flats and a new central railway station. A new Civic Centre and Town Hall was built on the West Park site that had been earmarked for it in the 1930s and opened in 1970. It was a successful building, contrasting effectively with the other, less distinctive post-war slabs that afflicted Sunderland and so many other towns.

In a rather halting and uncertain way the town was becoming more attractive, more pleasant to live in culturally as well as physically. The library and museum services so well founded in Victorian and Edwardian days were further extended, culminating in 1960–64 with the reorganization of the Central Library and Museum in much enlarged buildings. Other cultural activities flourished among a score of dramatic, musical, artistic and learned societies, all publicised and some partly financed by the Corporation. The Council's most substantial and rewarding venture in this field was its purchase in 1959 of the dying Empire Theatre and its

A multi-storey block of flats at Monkwearmouth

rehabilitation as a civic theatre offering at modest prices entertainment of a quality rarely equalled in a town of Sunderland's size and resources.

There was another side to the medal. New building implied extensive destruction in its wake. Few were concerned that many of the relics of Sunderland's industrial past and so much solid nineteenth-century housing had disappeared, for most of these had become derelict eyesores and two of the finest buildings, Ryhope Water Pumping Station and Monkwearmouth Railway Station, were fortunately preserved by local volunteers and civic interest to become museums. More were upset by the demolition of the former Town Hall in Fawcett Street, which seemed to show an unseemly readiness to destroy one of the few attractive relics of Sunderland's past. The Town Hall had been recognized as inadequate for the ever-multiplying functions of local government within a few years of its opening, but it was a building that had given Fawcett Street dignity and character and its loss perhaps implied that the street was no longer the commercial and administrative centre of the town.

Others were disturbed that the ever faster changes were not always for the better. Many of the town's churchmen felt doubt about their function in the new environment, a concern that found expression in the Bishop of Durham's commission of enquiry in 1970. New church-building had generally advanced with the new estates, though as the enquiry reported the demand had been sometimes miscalculated and overestimated, with the result that some of the new churches and halls, like the dingy stone buildings left behind by the demolition of so much of the older town, became neglected and a prey to the disturbing

The Town Hall. Opened in 1890, it was demolished in 1971

growth of vandalism. The Bishop's commission sought to suggest a new pattern and purpose for the churches in a twentieth-century urban environment.

There was some concern, too, over the nature and standards of education. Sunderland had long taken pride in its educational provision. The board schools of the 1870s had been gradually added to. The Technical College, favoured and financed by the town's employers as well as by the Corporation, had expanded its numbers, courses and buildings during the inter-war period. In the 1960s it grew again on a massive scale to become a splendidly equipped Polytechnic by 1969. A Training College for Teachers was established in 1908 and moved into Langham Tower, formerly a brewer's home, in 1922. A College of Arts and Crafts, moved to Backhouse Park in 1934 from its earlier home on the first floor of the Town Hall, was in 1969 absorbed into the Polytechnic.

The massive expansion of these institutions of higher education in the post-war period was equalled at the other end of the ladder by widespread building and re-equipment of primary schools. It was in the provision of secondary education that problems arose. Higher Grade Schools had been established as far back as 1891, becoming the Bede Collegiate Schools in 1905. Rehoused in modern buildings on the Durham Road in 1929, they had established high academic standards for their selected intake of pupils. Other secondary schools followed, and by 1955 they catered, with varying degrees of success, for all the children of the town. In that year the Council proposed the introduction of comprehensive schools, and in 1963 the first, Hylton Red House, was opened. But when it came to converting the existing grammar and modern schools difficulties were encountered. There was bitter political disagreement, distress over the sacrifice of tradition and quality, conflict with the government, changes of mind and confusion over the process of transition. There was much ill feeling and perhaps some lowering of educational standards; and by 1973 the future pattern of secondary education was still by no means clear.

Although some aspects of Sunderland's development gave cause for concern, in most respects life in the Sunderland of the early 1970s was good. Much, obviously, depended on outside and uncertain factors, on the future pattern of world trade, on the impact of the Common Market, on government development policies; but much, too, depended on the people of Sunderland and those they would find to lead them. They were soon to lose some of the trappings of their independent identity. In 1974, 1,300 years after Benedict Biscop founded his monastery on the muddy bank of the Wear and 138 years after the creation of the modern borough, Sunderland was destined to be merged in the new Metropolitan County of the Tyne and Wear, linked at last to its ancient rival.

TABLE OF RECENT DATES

1976, 20 April — Opening of Washington New Town Library

1978, 31 May — Crowtree Leisure Centre is officially opened by Prince Charles

1984, 30 March — The Japanese car maker, Nissan, announces that it will open a factory at Sunderland and construction of a multi-million pound plant ensues.

1984–85, 12 March to 3 March — Wearmouth and other local mines are disrupted by the bitter national miners' strike.

1986, 1 April — Sunderland's two remaining shipyards, Austin and Pickersgill and Sunderland Shipbuilders Ltd (both nationalized in 1977), merge to form North East Shipbuilders Ltd.

1988, 7 December — The government announces the closure of North East Shipbuilders Ltd. The decision results in the redundancy of around 2,000 shipyard workers and the end of a centuries-old industry in Sunderland.

1992, 23 March — Sunderland is granted city status by the Queen.

1992, 16 June — Sunderland Polytechnic becomes a university.

1993, 10 December — Wearmouth, the last mine in the Durham coalfield, closes with the loss of 670 jobs.

1995, 23 January — City Library opens in Fawcett Street. Previously known as Sunderland Central Library, it abandoned its Borough Road premises to move to its more spacious new location.

1997, 13 May — Sunderland AFC plays its last match at Roker Park prior to moving to the Stadium of Light.

1998, 23 October — The National Glass Centre is officially opened by Prince Charles.

1999, 2 July — Vaux Breweries, a local firm dating from the 19th century, closes with the loss of 430 jobs on Wearside.

2001, 29 June — Fulwell Mill, a well known Sunderland landmark dating from 1821, is officially opened by the leader of Sunderland City Council after being restored to working order.

2002, 31 March — The extension of the Tyne and Wear Metro to Sunderland opens.

2002, 7 May — The Winter Gardens are officially opened by the Queen.

2003, 26–27 July — Sunderland's fifteenth annual air show is held. The city's adopted ship, HMS *Ocean* (the largest vessel in the Royal Navy) anchors offshore before entering the harbour on the show's closing afternoon.

Note on Sources

I list here only those books and articles on which I have relied heavily. A fuller bibliography of Sunderland history is to be published shortly: H.G. Bowling and T. Corfe, *History in Sunderland: a Guide*.

1. General Histories

The Region

Smailes, A.E. *North England*, Nelson, 1960, 1968
Surtees, Robert *History and Antiquities of the County Palatine of Durham*, Nichols & Bentley (London) and Andrews (Durham), 1816–40
Mackenzie, E. and Ross, M. *Historical, Topographical and Descriptive View of the County Palatine of Durham*, Mackenzie & Dent, 1834
Fordyce, W. *History and Antiquities of the County Palatine of Durham*, Fullarton, 1857
Boyle, J.R. *The County of Durham, its Castles, Churches and Manor-Houses*, Walter Scott, 1892
Victoria History of the County of Durham, ed. Page, W., Constable/St Catherine's Press/OUP, 1905–28
Dewdney, J.C. (ed.) *Durham County and City with Teesside*, British Association, Durham, 1970

Sunderland

Garbutt, George *History of Monkwearmouth, Bishopwearmouth and Sunderland*, Garbutt, 1819
Burnett, J. *History of the Town and Port of Sunderland*, Burnett, 1830
Summers, J.W. *History and Antiquities of Sunderland*, vol. I, Joseph Tate, 1858
Potts, Taylor *Sunderland, a History of the Town, Port, Trade and Commerce*, B. Williams, 1892
Mitchell, W. Cranmer *History of Sunderland*, Hills, 1919, 1972
Sunderland Museum and Art Gallery, *Old Sunderland*, 1951, 1965
Bowling, H.G. (ed.) *Some Chapters on the History of Sunderland*, privately printed, 1969
Antiquities of Sunderland: Transactions of the Sunderland Antiquarian Society, occasional publication, 1900 on. Includes many articles of interest and value apart from those listed below.

2. Special Topics

These are listed roughly in the order in which they have been used in the text.
Bede, *Ecclesiastical History of the English Nation*, Everyman edition, Dent, 1910; includes *Lives of the Holy Abbots of Wearmouth and Jarrow*
Anon *The Life of Ceolfrid*, ed. Boutflower, D.S., Hills, 1912
Colgrave, B. and Cramp, R.J. *St Peter's Church, Wearmouth*, British Publishing Co., n.d.
Bruce-Mitford, R.L.S. 'The Art of the Codex Amiatinus', reprinted from *Journal of the Archaeological Association*, vol. XXXII, 1969

Nef, J.U. *The Rise of the British Coal-Trade*, Routledge, 1932
Robson, H.L. 'George Lilburne, Mayor of Sunderland', in *Ant. of Sunderland*, vol. XXII, 1960
Smith, J.W. and Holden, T.S. *Where Ships are Born*, Thomas Reed/Wear Shipbuilders Association, 1946, 1953
Miller, E. (ed.) *Eyewitness: the North East in the early Nineteenth Century*, Harold Hill for Sunderland College of Education, 1968
Walker, H.L. 'Ships, Sunderland and Lloyd's Register of Shipping' in *Durham County Local History Society Bulletin*, 12, 1970
Clarke, J.F. 'Labour in Shipbuilding on the North East Coast' in *Durham County Local History Society Bulletin*, 12, 1970
Robson, B.T. *Urban Analysis*, CUP, 1969
Dennis, Norman *People and Planning*, Faber, 1970

3. Publications that have appeared since 1973

Since *Sunderland–a Short History* was first published, the literature available has increased considerably and for the sake of brevity only some of this material is mentioned below.

Additional works by Tom Corfe himself include a useful booklet entitled *Wearside Heritage: a Guide to Sunderland*, 1975, and *Swan in Sunderland*, 1979, an account of the early life of the inventor Joseph Wilson Swan. Moreover, Corfe edited (and largely wrote) *The Buildings of Sunderland 1814–1914*, 1983; and co-wrote (with Geoffrey Milburn) *Buildings and Beliefs*, 1984.

A work of major importance (to which Tom Corfe contributed a fine chapter) is Geoffrey Milburn and Stuart Miller (eds.) *Sunderland, River, Town & People: a History from the 1780s to the Present Day*, 1988, whose authoritative text is accompanied by a wealth of illustrations and references. Much briefer, but nevertheless stimulating and also liberally endowed with illustrations, is Stuart Miller, *The Book of Sunderland*, 1989. Much more lavish is Carol Roberton, *Sunderland—the making of a 21st century city*, 2000, which has excellent photographs (many of them in colour) and a worthwhile text. The most recent general history is Glen Lyndon Dodds, *A History of Sunderland*, (2nd edition), 2001.

A number of publications dealing with specific localities have also been published. A notable contribution has been made by Peter Gibson, who has written several books on Southwick such as *Southwick-on-Wear: an Illustrated History*, 1985, and *Southwick: the People's History*, 1999.

Other publications on localities include: S. Holley, *Washington: Quicker by Quango, the history of Washington New Town 1964–1983*, 1983; four volumes published by Monkwearmouth Local History Society, beginning with *Monkwearmouth Memories vol. I*, 1989; M. Robinson, *Barbary Coasters: Memories of a Proud Sunderland Community*, 2001; D.W. Smith, *Herrington and its Folk*, 1987; and *South Hylton Recalled*, 2003, by South Hylton Local History Society.

Other relevant material includes:

Anderson, A., 'Sunderland's Part in the Colonization of Australia', *Sunderland's History 2000*, 2000
Baker, J.C., *Sunderland Pottery*, 1984
Brady, K., *Sunderland's Blitz*, 1999

Brett, A., and Royal, J., *Old Pubs of Sunderland*, 1993
Clarke, J.F., *Building Ships on the North East Coast: a Labour of Love, Risk and Pain*, 1997
Dodds, G.L., 'St Andrew's Church, Roker', *Durham Archaeological Journal* vol. 10, 1994
Dodds, G.L., 'The Prehistory of the Sunderland Area', *Sunderland's History 8*, 1995
Dodds, G.L., *Paley, Wearside & Natural Theology*, 2003
Hudson, J., and Callaghan, P., (eds.) *Sunderland AFC: the Official History 1879–2000*, 1999
James, J. G., *The Cast Iron Bridge at Sunderland*, 1986
Jessop, L., and Sinclair, N.T., *Sunderland Museum: the People's Palace in the Park*, 1996
Martin, P., *The Tom Cowie Story*, 1998
Milburn, G.E., *Church and Chapel in Sunderland 1780–1914*, 1988
Milburn, G.E., *Holy Trinity, Sunderland – an illustrated history and guide*, 1990
Milburn, G.E., 'John Hampson's Life of John Wesley', *Sunderland's History 2000*, 2000
Miller, S.T., 'The River Wear Commission 1717–1859', *Antiquities of Sunderland* vol. XXVII, 1977–1979
Miller, S.T., '"North Versus South": The Docks Dispute at Sunderland in the 1830s', *Industrial Archaeology Review*, vol. 4, no. 1, Winter 1979–80
Miller, S.T. and Brett, A., *Cholera in Sunderland*, 1992
Morley, B., *Hylton Castle*, 1979
Myers, B.A., *The Rectors of the ancient Parish Church of Bishopwearmouth 1195–1975*, 1975
Nicholson, P., *A Brewer at Bay, the Memoirs of Sir Paul Nicholson*, 2003
Patterson, G., 'Harrison's Buildings—Sunderland's first council housing', *Sunderland's History 3*, 1985
Potts, A., *Jack Casey: the Sunderland Assassin*, 1991
Potts, G.R., 'Frank Caws: Sunderland Architect', *Sunderland's History 10*, 2003
Sayers, A.B., *Sunderland Church High School for Girls: a centenary history 1884–1984*, 1984
Sinclair, N.T., *Railways of Sunderland*, 1985
Skempton, A.W., 'The Engineers of Sunderland Harbour, 1718–1817,' *Industrial Archaeology Review* vol. 1, no. 2, Spring 1977
Smith, D.W., *Out, All Out*, 1991, (a detailed account of the miners' strike at Silksworth in 1891)
Staddon, S.A., *Tramways of Sunderland*, 1991
Storey, P.J., 'Sunderland Newspapers', *Antiquities of Sunderland* vol. XXVII, 1977–1979
Turner, M.J., 'Reform Politics and the Sunderland By-Election of 1845', *Northern History* vol. XXXVIII, no.1, March 2001
Wheeler, D., 'Sunderland's Nineteenth Century Weather Observers', *Sunderland's History 7*, 1993

INDEX

Aethelfrith, king, 11
Aidan, St, 13, 14
Aldfrith, king, 15
Allan, J., 66
Alum, 24
Amity, 52
Andrews, E., 31
Anglo-Saxons, 11,13
Armyne, Sir W., 29
Assembly Garth, 45–46
Athelstan, king, 18
Athenaeum, 38
Austin's, shipbuilders, 51, 73, 83–84
Ayres, Robert, 24, 31

Ballast, 31, 57–58
Barnes Park, 28, 75
Barracks, 45
Bartram's, shipbuilders, 51, 83
Batteries, 45
Bede, 13, 15–16
Bede Schools, 88
Bede Tower, 38
Beefsteak Club, 43
Bellasyse, Sir W., 25–26
Bernicia, 11
Bible, 16
Biddick, 19
Biscop, Benedict, 13–15
Bishopwearmouth, 18, 20, 27, 35–36, 39; Rector of, 25, 35, 39, 43
Black, George, 80
Black Death, 20
Boldon, 18
Boldon Book, 18–19
Bombing, 66, 71, 80–81
Bonomi, I., 46
Bookselling, 44
Borgsten, 83
Borough, Puiset's, 19; Morton's, 25; modern, 41–42, 88
Boundaries, town, 77, 86
Bowes, Robert, 22–24
Bowes Quay, 24

Brandling Junction Railway, 57
Bridge, Alexandra, 69, 75
Bridge, Wear (1796), 36–37; (1929), 75
Brigantes, 8–9
Bronze Age, 8
Building (Bildon) Hill, 7, 18, 20, 35
Burdon, Rowland, 36–37
Burdon Road, 38
Burgage plots, 20
Burns, shipbuilders, 32
Burials, prehistoric, 8
bus services, 75

Candlish, J., 66
Carley Hill, 7, 10
Catholics, Roman, 22, 45–46
Cawdell, J., 45
Ceolfrith, 14–16
Chapels, 45–46
Charles I, king, 25
Charter, Puiset's, 19; Morton's, 25
Chester-le-Street, 28
Cholera epidemics, 39–41
Christ Church, 63
Christianity, 13
Church St, 33, 39
Churches, 45–46, 63–64, 87–88; see also Christ Church, Holy Trinity, St Andrew's, St John's, St Michael's, St Peter's
Church High Schools, 64
Cinema, 80
Civil War, 25–30
Clanny, W.R., 39–40, 43
Clarks engineers, 53
Cloisters, The, 38
Coal, 19, 22, 24, 29, 30–31, 55–57, 60, 69, 74, 84
Codex Amiatinus, 16
College, Art, 88; Technical, 69, 88; Training, 88
Copperas, 24
Corn Market Chapel, 46
Corporation Quay, 76
Cottages, 61–62

93

Cotterill, R., 26
Council, Borough, 41–42, 62–64, 66–68, 85–86
Court Line, 83
Cowan, Dr J., 45
Cox Green, 55
Crawford, Jack, 40
Crowley, Ambrose, 30
Crown's, shipbuilders, 51, 83

Davy, Sir H., 43
Debating Society, 43
Depression, 73–74, 78
Deptford, 24, 35–36, 39, 61
Diesel engines, 74
Docks, 58, 74, 85; North, 58; South, 58–59
Donnison School, 44
Doxford's, shipbuilders, 52–54, 72, 74, 82–83
Doxford Park, 86
Durham, Bishop of, 17–20
Durham & Sunderland Railway, 57, 59

Easington, 18
East Anglia, merchants of, 22–23
Ecclesiastical History of the English People, 16
Ecgfrith, king, 13
Echo, Sunderland, 67, 79
Education Act (1870), 64
Electricity, 64, 75
Elizabeth I, queen, 21, 22
Empire Theatre, 65, 80, 86–87
Engineering, marine, 53, 74
Esplanade, 38
Exchange, 41
Experiment, 52

farming, 8–9, 18–20
Fatfield, 19, 31, 55
Fawcett St, 37–38, 87
ferries, 36
fishing, 19–20, 76
Fitter's Row, 39
flats, multi-storey, 86
football, 66
Fothergill, R., 60
freemasons, 43–44
Freemen and stallingers, 33, 41, 48
Fulwell, 63, 78

Garbutt, G., 44
gas lighting and manufacture, 41
Gilley Law, 86
'Gladstone' Estate, 62
glass manufacture, 24, 35, 60
Golden Lion, 43
Goodchilds, 32, 50
Grange Crescent, 38
Grange School, 45
Greville, Charles, 40
Grimshaw, J., 60
Guardians, Board of, 47, 75

Halmote Court, 20
Harraton, 19, 23, 25
Harrison Buildings, 62
Hartley's, glassworks, 60
Hasting Hill, 7–8
Hat Case, 39
Hatfield, Bishop, 20
Havelock, Henry, 67
Havelock, Thomas, 50
Hendon, 11, 19–20, 62
Herrington, 11, 27, 86
Hetton, 56
Hetton Railway, 56, 84
High St, 20–21, 33, 39
Hilda, St, 14
Hind's Bridge, 18
Holy Trinity Church, 33–34
hospitals, 47–49, 71, 75
Hostmen, Company of, 22–24
Houghton-le-Spring, 7, 20
housing, 33, 61–63, 76–78, 81; council, 62, 77, 85–86
Howle-Eile Burn, 18
Hudson, George, 58–59
Humbledon Hill, 7, 8, 11, 42; Estate, 77
Hylton, 10, 36

Improvement Commissioners, 41
industrial estates, 79
industry, development of, 23–25, 30, 32, 35, 50–56, 60, 72, 79–80
infirmaries, 48–49
iron manufacture, 30
Irving, Henry, 65

James William St, 64
Jewish community, 46

Index

Jones, J. Paul, 45

keel-boats, 25, 31–32, 55
keelmen, 28, 30, 55–56

Labour Party, 78
La Hogue, 51
Laing's, shipbuilders, 51–52, 83
Lambton, 19, 23, 25
Lambton family, 22, 55
Leven, Lord, 26–28
Liberty ships, 82
Library, Circulating, 43; Subscription, 43; Town, 66, 69, 86
lighthouses, 31, 58, 76
Lilburne, George, 24–26, 29–30
Lilburne, John, 30
Lilburne, Robert, 29
lime-burning, 24, 32
Lloyd's Register, 50
local government, 25, 34–35, 41–42, 67, 78
Loftus, 52
Lord Duncan, 50
Low St, 20, 30
Lyceum Theatre, 65

Marley Potts, 77
mayors, 25, 41
Menvil, T., 20
Mesolithic, 8
Methodism, 46, 49
monks, 13–17, 21
Monkwearmouth, 8, 35, 51, 58, 85–86
Monkwearmouth Shore, 20, 35, 51, 62
Morton, Bishop, 25
Municipal Corporations Act (1835), 41
Murray's Handbook for Travellers, 63–64
Museum, 66, 86
music halls, 64–65

Naess Crusader, 84
Neolithic settlements, 8
Newbottle, 32; Waggonway, 56
Newcastle, 19–20, 22, 24, 26
Newcastle, Marquis of, 27–28
newspapers, 67
nonconformists, 45–46, 63–64
North Eastern Railway, 59
North Eastern Trading Estates, Ltd, 79
North Sands, 52, 83

Offerton, 23
Orenda Bridge, 84
Orphanage, 48
Osbourne, Graham & Co., 52

Palaeolithic peoples, 8
Paley, Archdeacon, 43
Pallion, 32, 52; Industrial Estate, 79
Panns, 23; Ferry, 36
Paramatta, 51
parks, 63, 75; Backhouse, 75; Barnes, 75; Mowbray, 63, 66, 71; Roker, 63
Parliament, Sunderland members of, 41, 58, 78
Pemberton, R. L., 60
Pennywell, 80
Pickersgill's, shipbuilders, 52, 83–84
piers, 31, 76
Phoenix Lodge, 43
place-names, 11
police, 42
Polytechnic, 88
Poor Law Amendment Act (1834), 47
population, 25, 33, 36, 61, 74
port, Sunderland as, 7, 19, 24, 30–31, 56–59, 76, 84
potteries, 32, 60
printing, 43–44
Public Assistance Committee, 75
Puiset, Bishop Hugh de, 18–19

Quakers, 44–46
quays, 24, 76

railways, 55–59, 85
Reform Act (1832), 41
River Wear Commissioners, 31, 57–59, 69, 75–76
road improvements, 75, 85
Roker, 63–64, 75, 78; Football Ground, 66
Romans, 8–10
Rome, 13
rope-making, 32, 60–61
Ryhope, 11, 86
Ryhope Rd, 38–39

St Andrew's Church, 64
St John's Chapel (Church), 45
St Mary's Church, 46
St Michael's Church, 18, 33

St Peter's Church, 14–17, 58
sailmaking, 32
salmon fisheries, 20
salt manufacture, 19, 23–24
Sans St, 33, 48
School Board, 64
schools, 34, 44–45, 64, 88
Seaburn, 75
seamen, 29, 39, 46–48, 60
sewage, 42
Sharp, Sir C., 43
shipbuilding, 20, 32, 50–54, 69, 71–74, 81–84, 89
shipwrights, 50–55
shopping centre, 86
Short's, shipbuilders, 52, 83
Silksworth, 32, 86
slums, 39, 42, 62, 76–77, 85
Smith, John, 23–24
South Shields, 24
Southwick, 36, 42, 58, 77
Springwell Estate, 85
staiths, 19, 22, 55–56, 84
steamships, 52–53
Stell Canch, 30–31
Stephenson, George, 56
Stephenson, Robert, 37
Storey, Samuel, 67, 79
Strike, General, 78–79
Sunderland, borough of (1835), 41–42; Earls of, 25; name, 15, 19; origins, 8, 13; parish of, 33–34, 39; port of, 19, 56–57, 74, 85; spread of, 32–33, 36–38, 61–63, 77, 85–86
Sunderland Society for the Prevention of Accidents . . ., 43
Sunderland Water Co., 42

Theatre Royal, 65
theatres, 45, 64–65
Thompson, J. L., shipbuilders, 52, 81–83
Thompson, Robert, shipbuilders, 52
Thorney Close, 85
Thornhill, J., 45
Times, The, 70
Torrens, 51–52
Town Hall, 41, 68, 86–87
Town Moor, 21, 33, 41, 45, 48
trade, 19, 24, 30–31, 57, 59, 70, 74, 84
Trafalgar Square Homes, 47–48
tramways, 64, 75

tugboats, 52, 58
Tunstall, 18; Hill, 7, 11
Tyne and Wear, Metropolitan County, 88

unemployment, 71, 73–75, 85

Valley Gardens, 63
Valley Road, 63
Vane-Tempest (Londonderry) family, 55–56, 59
Vaux's Brewery, 65, 89
Victoria Hall 66; disaster, 66
Vikings, 16

wages, shipyard workers, 55
waggonways, 56
War, First World, 71–72
War, Second World, 80–82
War Memorial, 71
Warwick, Earl of, 29
water supply, 42
Wear, River, 7–8, 20, 30–31, 57–58, 76
Wearmouth, 7, 13, 18, 19, 20; Colliery, 60, 74, 84, 89
Wesley, John, 46
Wheatsheaf, 71
Whitburn, 11
White, Andrew, 41
Williamson family, 35, 63; Sir Hedworth, 58, 62
Wilson, George, 45
Wilson, Thomas, 37
workhouses, 34, 46–47

Zeppelins, 71

Picture Credits

Edwin Mason, pages 63, 70
Newcastle Libraries & Information Service, pages 51, 53, 65
Tom Corfe, page 29
David Dodds, pages 76, 83
Gavin Dodds, pages 34, 48, 54, 61
Glen Lyndon Dodds, pages 38, 40, 42, 44, 59, 67, 78, 86
Shaun Dodds, cover & page 47
Sunderland Antiquarian Society, 35
Sunderland Echo, 87